SCIM in Identity Management

James Relington

DEDICATION

This book is dedicated to all the professionals working tirelessly to secure digital identities and protect organizations from ever-evolving threats. To the cybersecurity teams, IT administrators, and identity management experts who ensure safe and seamless access for users— your work is invaluable. And to my family and friends, whose support and encouragement made this journey possible, thank you.

AKNOWLEDGEMENTS

I would like to express my deepest gratitude to everyone who contributed to the creation of this book. To my colleagues and mentors in the cybersecurity and identity management field, your insights and expertise have been invaluable. To the organizations and professionals who shared their experiences and best practices, your contributions have enriched this work. A special thanks to my family and friends for their unwavering support and encouragement throughout this journey. Finally, to the readers, thank you for your interest in identity lifecycle management—may this book help you navigate the evolving landscape of digital security with confidence.

Introduction to SCIM

The System for Cross-domain Identity Management (SCIM) is a standardized protocol designed to simplify identity and access management across different systems. As organizations continue to adopt cloud-based applications and services, managing user identities efficiently has become increasingly complex. SCIM provides a unified approach for automating the exchange of user identity information between identity providers and service providers, reducing administrative overhead and improving security.

SCIM was created to address the challenges associated with provisioning and deprovisioning users in a distributed environment. Traditionally, user management required manual processes or custom integrations, leading to inefficiencies, inconsistencies, and security risks. With SCIM, organizations can ensure that user data remains synchronized across multiple platforms while reducing the need for manual intervention. The protocol defines a common schema for user attributes, making it easier for different systems to communicate and share identity information.

The need for SCIM became apparent as organizations moved toward Software-as-a-Service (SaaS) solutions and multi-cloud architectures. Each service provider typically has its own method for managing user identities, requiring custom scripts, API integrations, or manual processes to keep identity data consistent. This fragmentation introduces complexity, delays onboarding and offboarding processes, and increases the risk of outdated or orphaned accounts remaining active. By introducing a standardized approach, SCIM enables seamless identity synchronization across different systems, ensuring that user access remains up to date.

SCIM operates using RESTful APIs, making it highly compatible with modern web-based applications and services. It defines a set of endpoints that allow identity providers to create, update, delete, and retrieve user information in a structured format. This API-driven approach provides flexibility, scalability, and interoperability across various identity management solutions. Organizations can use SCIM to automate user provisioning and deprovisioning, enforce role-based access control, and maintain accurate identity records in real time.

One of the core benefits of SCIM is its ability to streamline user lifecycle management. When an employee joins a company, SCIM allows identity providers to automatically create a corresponding user account in all necessary applications and services. Similarly, when an employee leaves the organization, SCIM ensures that their access is revoked across all integrated systems, reducing the risk of unauthorized access. This automated approach not only enhances security but also improves efficiency by eliminating the need for manual updates.

Security is a fundamental aspect of SCIM. By providing a consistent and automated way to manage identity data, SCIM reduces the risk of misconfigurations and human errors that could lead to security breaches. The protocol supports authentication mechanisms such as OAuth 2.0 and relies on secure HTTPS communication to protect sensitive identity data during transmission. Additionally, SCIM enables organizations to implement strict access controls, ensuring that only authorized users and systems can modify identity information.

SCIM also promotes interoperability between different identity and access management (IAM) solutions. Because it follows a standardized schema, organizations can integrate SCIM with a wide range of applications, including cloud-based SaaS platforms, on-premises directories, and custom-built identity systems. This flexibility allows businesses to adopt new technologies without worrying about complex identity synchronization challenges. Service providers that implement SCIM can offer a seamless integration experience for their customers, improving adoption and reducing friction in identity management processes.

The adoption of SCIM has been driven by major technology companies and industry leaders who recognize the need for a standardized identity management solution. Many cloud service providers, including Google, Microsoft, and Okta, support SCIM in their identity management platforms, allowing organizations to integrate their existing identity infrastructure with external services. As SCIM continues to gain traction, more vendors are implementing support for the protocol, further increasing its relevance in modern identity management.

SCIM is not only useful for large enterprises but also benefits small and medium-sized businesses looking to enhance their identity management capabilities. By adopting SCIM, organizations of all sizes can reduce administrative burden, improve compliance with security policies, and ensure a consistent user experience across multiple applications. The ability to automate identity synchronization also helps IT teams focus on more strategic initiatives rather than spending time on routine user management tasks.

The flexibility of SCIM extends beyond just user provisioning. It also supports the management of groups, roles, and other identity-related attributes. Organizations can use SCIM to assign users to specific groups based on their roles, enforce access policies, and ensure that group memberships remain synchronized across different systems. This functionality is particularly valuable for enterprises that rely on role-based access control (RBAC) and need to maintain accurate access rights for employees, contractors, and partners.

As organizations continue to embrace digital transformation, the importance of efficient identity management cannot be overstated. SCIM provides a robust framework for managing user identities in an increasingly interconnected environment, ensuring that identity data remains accurate, secure, and up to date. By leveraging SCIM, businesses can enhance security, improve operational efficiency, and simplify the integration of identity management across diverse platforms.

The Evolution of Identity Management

Identity management has undergone a significant transformation over the past few decades. As technology has advanced, so too have the methods for managing user identities, access controls, and security. The shift from simple password-based authentication to sophisticated identity federation and cloud-based solutions reflects the growing need for secure, scalable, and efficient identity management systems. The evolution of identity management has been shaped by changes in computing environments, security threats, and regulatory requirements, leading to the development of modern identity frameworks such as SCIM.

In the early days of computing, identity management was a relatively simple concept. Users accessed mainframe systems through terminals, and authentication was typically handled with a basic username and password. User accounts were manually created and managed by IT administrators, often stored in a centralized directory or database. These systems, though limited in scope, were sufficient for the closed computing environments of the time. However, as organizations expanded their IT infrastructure and adopted distributed computing models, the limitations of traditional identity management approaches became apparent.

The rise of client-server architectures introduced new challenges for identity management. Organizations had to manage user accounts across multiple applications and systems, each with its own authentication mechanism. This led to an increase in password fatigue, as users were required to maintain multiple credentials for different systems. Additionally, IT departments faced an administrative burden in provisioning and deprovisioning accounts across various platforms, increasing the risk of security vulnerabilities such as orphaned accounts and inconsistent access controls.

The introduction of directory services, such as LDAP (Lightweight Directory Access Protocol) in the 1990s, marked a significant step forward in identity management. Directory services provided a structured way to store and retrieve user identity information, enabling centralized authentication and access control. Organizations could now manage user identities more efficiently by integrating applications with a central directory, reducing redundancy and improving security. However, LDAP-based systems were still largely on-premises solutions, requiring manual configuration and maintenance by IT teams.

As businesses embraced the internet and web-based applications, the limitations of traditional identity management approaches became more pronounced. The need for federated identity management arose as users required seamless access to multiple applications across different domains. Standards such as SAML (Security Assertion Markup Language) and OpenID emerged to facilitate identity federation, allowing users to authenticate once and gain access to multiple services without needing separate credentials for each one.

These advancements laid the foundation for modern single sign-on (SSO) solutions, which improved both security and user experience.

The shift to cloud computing brought further challenges and opportunities for identity management. With organizations increasingly relying on Software-as-a-Service (SaaS) applications, identity management had to evolve to support cloud-based environments. Traditional on-premises directory services were no longer sufficient, as users needed to authenticate across cloud and hybrid environments. Identity as a Service (IDaaS) solutions emerged to address this need, providing cloud-based identity management platforms that integrated with various applications and services.

During this period, identity and access management (IAM) frameworks expanded to incorporate multi-factor authentication (MFA), risk-based authentication, and adaptive access controls. Security threats such as phishing, credential theft, and insider attacks drove the adoption of stronger authentication mechanisms. Organizations recognized that passwords alone were not enough to protect sensitive data, leading to widespread adoption of MFA, which required users to verify their identity using multiple factors such as biometrics, security tokens, or one-time passcodes.

Regulatory and compliance requirements further influenced the evolution of identity management. Laws such as the General Data Protection Regulation (GDPR), the California Consumer Privacy Act (CCPA), and industry-specific regulations mandated stricter controls over user data and access management. Organizations had to implement robust identity governance processes, ensuring that user identities were properly managed, audited, and secured. This regulatory landscape reinforced the need for automated identity provisioning and deprovisioning, reducing human errors and enforcing compliance policies.

With the growing complexity of identity management, automation and standardization became critical. SCIM (System for Cross-domain Identity Management) emerged as a standardized protocol to streamline identity provisioning and synchronization across different systems. By defining a common schema and RESTful APIs, SCIM enabled organizations to automate user account management across cloud applications, directories, and identity providers. This development simplified identity integration efforts and reduced the administrative overhead associated with managing identities at scale.

The concept of Zero Trust security further transformed identity management in recent years. Traditional perimeter-based security models assumed that users inside the network were inherently trusted, but the increasing prevalence of remote work, mobile devices, and cloud services challenged this assumption. Zero Trust principles require continuous verification of user identities, device health, and contextual factors before granting access. Identity management solutions now incorporate real-time risk assessment and dynamic access policies to enforce Zero Trust security models, enhancing protection against cyber threats.

As artificial intelligence (AI) and machine learning technologies advance, identity management continues to evolve. AI-driven identity analytics can detect anomalous behavior, identify potential security risks, and automate identity lifecycle management. Organizations are increasingly leveraging AI to enhance identity governance, streamline access reviews, and enforce least-privilege access policies. These innovations are shaping the future of identity management, making it more intelligent, adaptive, and resilient.

The evolution of identity management reflects the ongoing need for secure and efficient ways to manage user identities and access. From the early days of manual account management to the emergence of cloud-based identity solutions and Zero Trust architectures, identity management has continuously adapted to meet the demands of modern computing environments. With the continued expansion of digital ecosystems, identity management will remain a fundamental aspect of cybersecurity, driving the adoption of new standards, technologies, and best practices.

Why SCIM?

Identity management has become a critical aspect of modern IT infrastructure, particularly as organizations increasingly rely on cloud services, Software-as-a-Service (SaaS) applications, and hybrid environments. Managing user identities across multiple platforms presents significant challenges, including manual provisioning, security risks, and compliance complexities. The System for Cross-domain Identity Management (SCIM) was developed to address these issues, providing a standardized framework for automating identity provisioning and synchronization across different systems. By reducing administrative overhead, improving security, and ensuring data consistency, SCIM simplifies identity management for organizations of all sizes.

One of the main reasons SCIM is necessary is the inefficiency of traditional user provisioning methods. Before SCIM, organizations relied on manual processes or custom-built scripts to create, update, and deactivate user accounts in different applications. These approaches were not only time-consuming but also prone to human error. An IT administrator had to ensure that new employees received the appropriate access to all necessary applications, often requiring separate credentials for each system. When employees left the company, administrators needed to manually remove access across various platforms, increasing the risk of orphaned accounts that could be exploited by malicious actors. SCIM eliminates these inefficiencies by automating identity lifecycle management, ensuring that user accounts are created and deactivated in real time.

Security is another key factor driving the adoption of SCIM. Orphaned accounts, inconsistent user permissions, and delays in deprovisioning pose serious security risks to organizations. Attackers often exploit dormant accounts to gain unauthorized access to systems, leading to data breaches and compliance violations. By implementing SCIM, organizations can ensure that user accounts remain synchronized across all platforms, reducing the likelihood of unauthorized access. When a user leaves an organization or changes roles, their access is updated instantly across all connected services, minimizing the risk of privilege escalation or account misuse.

SCIM also plays a crucial role in regulatory compliance. Regulations such as the General Data Protection Regulation (GDPR), the California Consumer Privacy Act (CCPA), and various industry-specific security standards require organizations to maintain strict control over user data and access permissions. Companies must be able to demonstrate that they are managing identities securely and efficiently, with clear audit trails of user access changes. SCIM provides a standardized way to enforce access control policies and generate logs of identity-related actions, making it easier to comply with security and privacy regulations. Organizations that fail to properly manage user identities risk fines, legal repercussions, and reputational damage.

Scalability is another major reason why SCIM is essential. As businesses grow, so does the complexity of identity management. Organizations with thousands or even millions of users must be able to efficiently manage identity synchronization across numerous applications. Without SCIM, IT teams must rely on custom integration solutions that may not scale effectively as new applications and users are added. SCIM's standardized schema and RESTful API framework enable seamless scalability, allowing organizations to expand their identity management capabilities without requiring extensive manual effort. This is particularly important for enterprises operating in multi-cloud and hybrid environments, where identity management needs to span multiple service providers.

Another advantage of SCIM is its ability to improve the user experience. Employees, customers, and partners expect seamless access to the applications they use daily. Without SCIM, users may need to create separate accounts for each service, leading to password fatigue and increased support requests due to forgotten credentials. SCIM enables single sign-on (SSO) and centralized authentication by synchronizing user identities across different platforms. This means users can access all necessary applications with a single set of credentials, improving convenience and reducing friction in the authentication process. A smooth user experience is especially important for SaaS providers, who rely on SCIM to simplify onboarding and enhance customer satisfaction.

The flexibility of SCIM makes it a valuable tool for a wide range of use cases. Enterprises use SCIM to integrate their internal identity providers with external applications, ensuring that employees have the right access to productivity tools, HR systems, and collaboration platforms. SaaS providers implement SCIM to allow their customers to integrate seamlessly with identity providers such as Microsoft Entra ID, Okta, and Google Workspace. Educational institutions use SCIM to manage student and faculty identities across learning management systems, email platforms, and research databases. The ability to automate identity provisioning across diverse environments makes SCIM a critical component of modern IT infrastructures.

SCIM's adoption is further driven by its alignment with other modern identity standards. It works in conjunction with protocols such as OAuth 2.0, OpenID Connect, and SAML to enable secure authentication and authorization. By integrating SCIM with these technologies, organizations can create a comprehensive identity and access management (IAM) strategy that enhances security while reducing complexity. Unlike proprietary identity management solutions that lock organizations into vendor-specific ecosystems, SCIM is an open standard, promoting interoperability between different identity systems. This ensures that organizations are not dependent on a single vendor for identity management, giving them the flexibility to switch providers as needed.

Cloud computing has accelerated the need for SCIM. As businesses migrate workloads to the cloud, they require a way to manage user identities across on-premises directories and cloud-based applications. Hybrid environments introduce additional complexity, as organizations must synchronize user data between legacy systems and modern cloud services. SCIM bridges this gap by providing a common identity management framework that supports both on-premises and cloud-based identity providers. This makes it easier for organizations to adopt cloud technologies while maintaining control over user identities and access.

The growing threat of cyberattacks has made effective identity management more important than ever. Phishing, credential stuffing, and insider threats continue to pose significant risks to organizations of all sizes. A well-implemented SCIM strategy helps mitigate these risks by ensuring that access permissions are updated in real time and that accounts are deactivated as soon as they are no longer needed. Automating identity management reduces the potential for human error, which is often a leading cause of security breaches. Organizations that prioritize identity automation through SCIM gain a stronger security posture and a more resilient IT environment.

SCIM addresses many of the challenges organizations face when managing user identities in today's complex digital landscape. By standardizing identity provisioning and synchronization, it reduces administrative burden, enhances security, ensures compliance, and improves the user experience. As cloud adoption continues to rise and cybersecurity threats become more sophisticated, SCIM remains a vital tool for organizations looking to streamline identity management while maintaining strong security controls. The widespread adoption of SCIM by leading technology companies and service providers demonstrates its value in modern IT ecosystems, making it an essential component of identity and access management strategies.

SCIM Architecture Overview

The System for Cross-domain Identity Management (SCIM) is designed to streamline identity management by providing a standardized framework for provisioning, updating, and deprovisioning user identities across multiple systems. Its architecture is based on a RESTful API model that ensures interoperability between identity providers and service providers, making it an essential tool for organizations managing user identities across cloud-based and on-premises applications. The SCIM architecture consists of various components that work together to facilitate identity synchronization while maintaining security, scalability, and efficiency.

At the core of SCIM is the concept of resource management. SCIM defines users and groups as primary resources, each with a set of attributes that adhere to a standardized schema. This schema allows identity providers and service providers to communicate using a common language, reducing the need for custom integrations. The SCIM schema includes attributes such as usernames, emails, phone numbers, roles, and group memberships, ensuring consistency in identity representation across different systems. The ability to extend this schema also provides flexibility for organizations with unique identity requirements.

SCIM operates through two main roles: the SCIM provider and the SCIM consumer. The SCIM provider, also known as the identity provider, is responsible for storing and managing user identities. This could be an enterprise directory service, a cloud-based identity provider, or a custom identity management system. The SCIM consumer, often referred to as the service provider, is the application or service that requires identity data to grant or restrict user access. These two roles communicate through standardized SCIM endpoints, allowing seamless identity synchronization without requiring direct database access.

The communication between SCIM providers and consumers is facilitated through RESTful API calls. SCIM endpoints follow a structured URL format that allows identity data to be created, retrieved, updated, or deleted. The API follows standard HTTP methods, with POST used for creating new resources, GET for retrieving existing resources, PUT and PATCH for updating user attributes, and DELETE for removing accounts or group memberships. This consistency in API design enables service providers to integrate SCIM with minimal effort, improving automation and reducing operational complexity.

Filtering, sorting, and pagination are integral aspects of SCIM's architecture. Since identity providers may manage thousands or even millions of user records, efficient querying mechanisms are necessary to optimize data retrieval. SCIM supports filtering using expressions that allow consumers to request only specific user records that meet defined criteria. Sorting ensures that results are ordered according to specified attributes, while pagination prevents excessive data transfers by limiting the number of records returned in a single request. These features contribute to the overall scalability of SCIM, making it suitable for large-scale deployments.

One of the strengths of SCIM is its support for bulk operations. In large organizations, identity updates often involve modifying multiple user accounts simultaneously. SCIM provides a bulk API endpoint that allows multiple operations to be processed in a single request. This reduces the number of API calls required for provisioning or updating users, improving efficiency and performance. Bulk operations are particularly useful for onboarding or offboarding employees, where multiple accounts need to be created or removed within a short timeframe.

Security is a fundamental component of SCIM's architecture. Identity data is highly sensitive, and ensuring its protection is a priority. SCIM relies on secure authentication mechanisms such as OAuth 2.0 and relies on encrypted HTTPS connections to prevent unauthorized access to identity records. Additionally, SCIM implementations can enforce access controls to ensure that only authorized applications can modify or retrieve identity data. Organizations implementing SCIM must follow security best practices, such as token-based authentication, role-based access control, and audit logging to track identity changes.

SCIM's extensibility allows organizations to tailor it to their specific identity management needs. While SCIM defines a standardized schema for users and groups, it also provides the ability to introduce custom attributes. This flexibility enables businesses to include additional identity-related information that may not be covered by the default schema. Custom attributes can be used to store job titles, department names, authentication methods, or other organization-specific data. However, maintaining consistency across extensions is essential to avoid interoperability issues with third-party SCIM consumers.

The role of SCIM in hybrid cloud environments is increasingly important. Many enterprises operate a mix of on-premises identity directories and cloud-based SaaS applications, requiring a seamless way to synchronize identities between these systems. SCIM acts as a bridge between legacy directories such as Active Directory and modern identity providers, ensuring that user identities remain consistent regardless of where authentication occurs. This integration capability is crucial for organizations transitioning to cloud-based identity solutions while maintaining compatibility with existing infrastructure.

SCIM adoption continues to grow among SaaS providers seeking to enhance their identity integration capabilities. By implementing SCIM, service providers can offer their customers an automated way to synchronize users and groups from external identity providers. This reduces the burden on IT teams who would otherwise have to manage user accounts manually. Additionally, SCIM allows organizations to enforce access policies dynamically, ensuring that users have the appropriate permissions based on their current role or department.

The standardization introduced by SCIM simplifies identity federation across multiple platforms. Before SCIM, organizations relied on proprietary APIs and custom scripts to integrate identity management solutions, leading to inconsistencies and high maintenance costs. SCIM eliminates these challenges by providing a universally accepted framework that works across different vendors and technologies. This standardization accelerates deployment times and reduces the complexity associated with identity synchronization, making it an essential component of modern identity and access management strategies.

SCIM architecture is designed to be both scalable and future-proof. As organizations continue to expand their digital ecosystems, identity management requirements will evolve. SCIM's modular architecture ensures that it can adapt to new identity technologies, authentication mechanisms, and security frameworks. The protocol's reliance on RESTful APIs and JSON-based data structures makes it highly compatible with modern web applications, ensuring its relevance as identity management needs grow more complex. Organizations that adopt SCIM benefit from a flexible, automated, and secure identity management solution that streamlines user provisioning and synchronization across an ever-expanding digital landscape.

Understanding SCIM Protocol

The System for Cross-domain Identity Management (SCIM) protocol was designed to standardize the management of user identities across multiple systems and services. As organizations adopt more cloud-based applications and distributed environments, the need for an efficient and secure way to synchronize identity data has become critical. SCIM provides a simple, automated approach to identity provisioning, ensuring that user information remains consistent across identity providers and service providers without requiring manual intervention.

SCIM follows a RESTful API model, allowing applications to communicate over HTTP using well-defined endpoints. The protocol is structured around resources, with users and groups being the primary entities managed by SCIM. Each resource is represented using a standardized JSON schema, which defines attributes such as usernames, emails, roles, and group memberships. This structured approach ensures interoperability between different identity management solutions, reducing the complexity of integrating identity providers with external applications.

One of the core principles of SCIM is to provide a common framework for provisioning and deprovisioning users. When a new employee joins an organization, SCIM allows the identity provider to automatically create a corresponding user account in all connected applications. Similarly, when an employee leaves, SCIM ensures that their access is revoked across all integrated systems in real-time. This automation minimizes security risks associated with orphaned accounts and reduces the administrative workload on IT teams.

SCIM endpoints follow a predictable URL structure, making it easier for developers to implement and maintain integrations. Each resource type, such as users and groups, has a designated endpoint that supports various HTTP methods. A POST request is used to create new user accounts, while GET retrieves user information. Updates to user attributes are handled using PUT or PATCH, depending on whether a complete or partial update is required. DELETE removes user accounts or group memberships as necessary. These standard operations provide a uniform way to manage identity data across different platforms.

Filtering, sorting, and pagination are essential features of the SCIM protocol that optimize data retrieval. Large enterprises often manage thousands or even millions of user records, requiring efficient querying mechanisms. SCIM supports filtering using logical expressions, allowing consumers to request specific user records based on attributes such as email addresses, department names, or job titles. Sorting enables results to be ordered based on specified fields, while pagination limits the number of records returned in a single request to improve performance. These capabilities enhance scalability and ensure that identity synchronization remains efficient even in large-scale environments.

SCIM provides support for bulk operations, enabling multiple user accounts to be created, updated, or deleted in a single request. This is particularly useful during onboarding, where large numbers of employees need access to corporate applications at once. Instead of making separate API calls for each user, SCIM allows organizations to perform bulk modifications, significantly reducing processing time and network overhead. Bulk operations also improve consistency by ensuring that identity updates are applied uniformly across all affected accounts.

Security is a fundamental aspect of SCIM, as it involves the exchange of sensitive identity data. The protocol enforces authentication mechanisms such as OAuth 2.0 to ensure that only authorized clients can access SCIM endpoints. Additionally, all communication between SCIM providers and consumers occurs over encrypted HTTPS connections, preventing unauthorized access or data interception. Organizations implementing SCIM must follow best practices for access control, including enforcing role-based permissions and maintaining audit logs of identity-related transactions.

SCIM's extensibility allows organizations to customize its functionality to meet specific identity management requirements. While the protocol defines a core schema for users and groups, it also supports extensions that enable additional attributes to be included in identity records. This flexibility ensures that SCIM can accommodate industry-specific identity requirements, such as healthcare organizations needing to track professional certifications or financial institutions managing compliance-related user attributes. However, maintaining interoperability across different SCIM implementations requires careful management of custom extensions to avoid compatibility issues.

SCIM facilitates integration with other identity management standards, enhancing its effectiveness in modern IT environments. It works alongside protocols such as SAML for single sign-on (SSO) and OpenID Connect for federated authentication. By integrating SCIM with these technologies, organizations can create a unified identity and access management (IAM) framework that supports both authentication and provisioning. This synergy allows organizations to streamline user access while ensuring that identity data remains synchronized across all systems.

The adoption of SCIM has been driven by major technology companies and cloud service providers, who recognize the benefits of standardized identity management. Leading SaaS providers have implemented SCIM support to simplify user provisioning for their customers, reducing the need for manual account creation and maintenance. Enterprises that implement SCIM benefit from faster onboarding, reduced administrative overhead, and improved security posture. As more organizations embrace cloud computing and hybrid environments, the demand for SCIM continues to grow, reinforcing its importance in modern identity management strategies.

SCIM plays a critical role in hybrid identity environments, where organizations maintain a mix of on-premises directories and cloud-based applications. Traditional directory services such as Active Directory were not designed for seamless integration with cloud services, leading to identity fragmentation. SCIM acts as a bridge between legacy identity systems and modern cloud platforms, ensuring that user data remains consistent across both environments. This capability is especially valuable for organizations transitioning to cloud-based identity solutions while maintaining interoperability with existing infrastructure.

The protocol's design prioritizes simplicity and ease of implementation, making it accessible to developers and IT administrators. Unlike proprietary identity management solutions that require extensive customization, SCIM provides a standardized, vendor-neutral approach to identity synchronization. Its lightweight architecture and reliance on RESTful APIs make it well-suited for cloud-based applications, enabling rapid deployment and seamless integration with existing identity providers. Organizations looking to modernize their identity management practices can adopt SCIM without the complexity associated with traditional identity provisioning methods.

SCIM's role in improving user experience is another key factor in its widespread adoption. Employees and customers expect seamless access to applications without unnecessary authentication barriers. Without SCIM, users may need to create separate accounts for each service, leading to password fatigue and increased support requests. SCIM simplifies this process by automatically provisioning user accounts based on existing identity data, ensuring that users can access necessary applications without delays or redundant credential management. This enhances productivity while reducing frustration associated with fragmented authentication processes.

As cybersecurity threats continue to evolve, organizations must prioritize robust identity management practices to protect sensitive data. Threats such as account takeovers, insider attacks, and credential stuffing require proactive identity security measures. SCIM helps mitigate these risks by enforcing real-time identity updates and ensuring that access permissions remain accurate. Automated provisioning and deprovisioning reduce the likelihood of unauthorized access, strengthening an organization's overall security posture. By implementing SCIM, organizations can maintain greater control over identity management while enhancing operational efficiency.

SCIM 1.1 vs SCIM 2.0

The System for Cross-domain Identity Management (SCIM) was developed to simplify the provisioning and synchronization of user identities across different applications and services. As the adoption of cloud computing and SaaS applications increased, organizations required a standardized method to manage user identities efficiently. The first widely adopted version, SCIM 1.1, provided the foundation for automated identity provisioning, but it also had limitations that prompted the development of SCIM 2.0. The evolution from SCIM 1.1 to SCIM 2.0 introduced significant improvements in flexibility, security, and standardization, making the protocol more robust for modern identity management needs.

SCIM 1.1 was designed to address the challenges of identity synchronization across different systems. It introduced a simple REST-based approach that allowed identity providers and service providers to exchange user and group data in a structured format. By defining a standard schema for users and groups, SCIM 1.1 enabled organizations to move away from proprietary identity management solutions and custom integration scripts. This early version provided basic capabilities such as user creation, updates, and deletions but lacked extensibility and suffered from inconsistencies in implementation.

One of the major issues with SCIM 1.1 was the rigidity of its schema. While it defined a common structure for user and group objects, it did not offer a flexible way to extend attributes. Organizations often needed to store additional identity-related information that was not covered by the SCIM 1.1 schema, but the lack of a clear extension mechanism forced them to rely on custom implementations. This led to interoperability challenges between different SCIM implementations, as each vendor handled schema extensions differently.

SCIM 1.1 also had inconsistencies in how attributes were handled across different service providers. The specification did not enforce strict rules for attribute naming, formatting, or validation, leading to variations in how user data was processed. Some implementations required attributes to be formatted in a specific way, while others used different conventions, making it difficult to achieve seamless interoperability. These inconsistencies created additional complexity for organizations trying to integrate SCIM with multiple service providers.

To address the shortcomings of SCIM 1.1, the SCIM working group introduced SCIM 2.0, which significantly improved the protocol's extensibility, standardization, and security. One of the most notable changes in SCIM 2.0 was the introduction of a more flexible schema extension model. Instead of forcing organizations to rely on proprietary modifications, SCIM 2.0 defined a structured approach to extending attributes. This allowed identity providers and service providers to introduce custom attributes while maintaining compatibility with the core SCIM specification.

SCIM 2.0 also introduced a more robust resource model. While SCIM 1.1 focused primarily on users and groups, SCIM 2.0 expanded the concept of resources to allow for greater flexibility. This meant that organizations could define additional resource types beyond users and groups, making SCIM 2.0 more adaptable to various identity management scenarios. The ability to manage custom resources allowed organizations to synchronize not only individual user accounts but also more complex identity structures such as roles, entitlements, and permissions.

Another major improvement in SCIM 2.0 was its refined API operations. SCIM 1.1 had inconsistencies in how API requests were processed, leading to variations in implementation across different service providers. SCIM 2.0 established clear guidelines for handling HTTP methods such as POST, GET, PUT, PATCH, and DELETE, ensuring that identity data could be managed consistently. The introduction of PATCH requests was particularly important, as it allowed partial updates to user records instead of requiring a full resource replacement. This improvement reduced unnecessary data transfers and improved efficiency in identity synchronization.

Filtering and querying capabilities were also enhanced in SCIM 2.0. While SCIM 1.1 provided basic filtering options, it lacked advanced querying features that organizations needed to efficiently manage large datasets. SCIM 2.0 introduced more powerful filtering expressions, allowing identity providers to retrieve users and groups based on multiple attribute conditions. This made it easier to perform targeted queries, such as searching for users based on department, role, or last login activity. These advanced filtering options improved performance and reduced the need for custom query logic.

Security was another area where SCIM 2.0 introduced significant enhancements. SCIM 1.1 relied on basic authentication mechanisms, which were not always sufficient for protecting sensitive identity data. SCIM 2.0 explicitly recommended the use of OAuth 2.0 for authentication and authorization, ensuring that API requests were securely controlled. The use of OAuth 2.0 tokens improved security by enforcing stricter access controls, reducing the risk of unauthorized access to identity data. Additionally, SCIM 2.0 required that all communications occur over HTTPS to protect data in transit from interception or tampering.

Error handling and response codes were also improved in SCIM 2.0. In SCIM 1.1, error messages were not consistently formatted, making it difficult for developers to diagnose issues when integrating SCIM with different services. SCIM 2.0 introduced a standardized approach to error responses, providing clear status codes and descriptive error messages. This made troubleshooting easier and improved the overall reliability of SCIM integrations.

Another important refinement in SCIM 2.0 was the standardization of bulk operations. SCIM 1.1 introduced basic support for bulk operations, allowing multiple users to be created or updated in a single request. However, the implementation lacked consistency, leading to variations in how different service providers handled bulk requests. SCIM 2.0 established a more structured approach to bulk operations, ensuring that large-scale identity updates could be performed efficiently while maintaining data integrity.

The adoption of SCIM 2.0 has been widespread among technology providers, identity management platforms, and SaaS applications. Major cloud service providers have embraced SCIM 2.0 as the preferred standard for identity synchronization due to its flexibility and improved security. Organizations implementing SCIM today typically adopt SCIM 2.0 rather than SCIM 1.1, as it offers better compatibility, stronger security measures, and more efficient identity provisioning capabilities.

SCIM 2.0 represents a significant advancement over SCIM 1.1, addressing many of the limitations that organizations faced with the earlier version. The improvements in schema flexibility, API consistency, security, and error handling make SCIM 2.0 a more reliable and scalable solution for identity management. As organizations continue to expand their digital ecosystems, the adoption of SCIM 2.0 ensures that identity provisioning remains seamless, secure, and efficient across a wide range of applications and services.

Core SCIM Resources

The System for Cross-domain Identity Management (SCIM) provides a standardized way to manage user identities across different systems and applications. At the heart of SCIM are its core resources, which define the objects that can be created, modified, and retrieved using the SCIM protocol. These resources establish a structured framework for identity synchronization, ensuring that identity providers and service providers can exchange user and group information in a consistent manner. SCIM's resource model is designed to be extensible, allowing organizations to manage identity data efficiently while maintaining interoperability with other SCIM-compliant systems.

The User resource is one of the fundamental building blocks of SCIM. It represents an individual user within an identity management system and contains attributes that define their identity, access rights, and contact information. A SCIM user record includes attributes such as usernames, emails, display names, phone numbers, and roles. The structured nature of the User resource ensures that identity data remains consistent across different platforms, reducing the complexity of user provisioning. Each user is assigned a unique identifier, allowing identity providers to track and update user records without ambiguity.

SCIM users also include metadata that provides information about when the user record was created, last modified, or deactivated. This metadata ensures that identity changes are properly tracked and that user records remain up to date across integrated systems. Organizations can use SCIM to automate changes to user attributes based on role changes, department transfers, or security policies. By synchronizing user identities through SCIM, IT teams can ensure that employees have the appropriate access rights to applications and services without requiring manual intervention.

The Group resource is another key component of SCIM. Groups define collections of users who share common access privileges, making them a crucial element of role-based access control (RBAC) and policy enforcement. A SCIM group consists of a unique identifier, a display name, and a list of member users. Groups simplify access management by allowing administrators to assign permissions at the group level rather than individually configuring access for each user. This approach improves efficiency and ensures consistency in access control policies.

Groups in SCIM are often used to manage team structures, project assignments, and application access levels. For example, an organization might create groups such as "Marketing Team," "IT Support," or "Administrators," each with predefined access to specific systems. When a new employee joins a department, they can be added to the relevant SCIM group, automatically granting them the necessary permissions. Likewise, when a user is removed from a group, their access to associated applications is revoked, reducing the risk of unauthorized access.

SCIM allows for dynamic and static group memberships. Static groups have manually assigned members, where administrators specify which users belong to a particular group. Dynamic groups, on the other hand, use rules and attributes to determine membership automatically. This capability is particularly useful in large organizations where managing individual group assignments manually would be impractical. By leveraging attribute-based group memberships, organizations can enforce consistent access policies without requiring continuous administrative oversight.

The Service Provider Configuration resource provides essential details about a SCIM implementation, allowing clients to understand the capabilities of a given SCIM service. This resource includes information about supported authentication mechanisms, schema extensions, and API versions. When an identity provider connects to a SCIM service, it can query the Service Provider Configuration resource to determine which features are available. This ensures that SCIM clients and servers can establish compatibility before exchanging identity data.

Another important resource within SCIM is the Schema resource, which defines the attributes and structure of other SCIM resources. Each SCIM implementation adheres to a predefined schema that specifies the attributes associated with users, groups, and custom extensions. The Schema resource allows identity providers to extend SCIM with additional attributes while maintaining compatibility with the core specification. By defining attribute constraints, data types, and validation rules, the Schema resource ensures consistency in how identity information is stored and exchanged.

SCIM also includes the Resource Type resource, which describes the different types of resources supported by a SCIM service. This resource helps clients understand the available SCIM objects and their associated schemas. By querying the Resource Type resource, identity providers can dynamically adapt to different SCIM implementations without requiring hardcoded configurations. This flexibility allows SCIM to support a wide range of identity management scenarios while maintaining a consistent protocol structure.

Each SCIM resource follows a RESTful architecture, allowing identity management operations to be performed using standard HTTP methods. Creating a new user or group involves sending a POST request to the appropriate SCIM endpoint, while retrieving user data requires a GET request. Updating user attributes can be achieved through PUT or PATCH operations, depending on whether a full or partial update is needed. Deleting a user or group is done using a DELETE request, ensuring that identity data remains accurate and up to date across all connected systems.

SCIM's core resources are designed to support identity management at scale. Organizations that manage large user populations can leverage SCIM's filtering, sorting, and pagination features to optimize performance. For example, an enterprise with thousands of employees can retrieve only the user records that match specific criteria, such as users from a particular department or users with a specific role. Pagination allows for efficient data retrieval by limiting the number of records returned in a single request, reducing network load and improving response times.

The extensibility of SCIM resources makes them adaptable to a wide range of identity management needs. While SCIM provides a standardized schema for users and groups, organizations can extend these resources to accommodate additional identity attributes. Custom extensions can be used to store department-specific information, compliance attributes, or authentication preferences. This flexibility allows SCIM to be used across different industries, including finance, healthcare, and education, each of which may have unique identity management requirements.

SCIM resources play a central role in automating identity provisioning and synchronization across enterprise applications. By defining a standardized set of objects for managing users, groups, and configurations, SCIM simplifies identity integration between identity providers and service providers. The structured nature of SCIM resources ensures that identity data remains consistent, secure, and interoperable across different platforms. Organizations that implement SCIM can reduce the administrative burden of managing user identities while improving security and compliance in an increasingly complex IT landscape.

User and Group Management with SCIM

User and group management is a fundamental aspect of identity and access management, ensuring that individuals have the correct access to applications, systems, and resources. The System for Cross-domain Identity Management (SCIM) standardizes this process by providing a structured and automated approach to provisioning, updating, and deprovisioning users and groups across different platforms. By leveraging SCIM, organizations can achieve consistent identity synchronization, improve security, and reduce administrative overhead.

SCIM defines users as individual identity objects that contain essential attributes such as usernames, emails, phone numbers, roles, and other relevant identity details. Each user within a SCIM system has a unique identifier, allowing identity providers and service providers to track changes and updates efficiently. The structured schema ensures that user data remains consistent, making it easier to manage identities across multiple applications without the need for manual interventions or custom integrations.

User creation in SCIM follows a standardized process using a RESTful API. When a new employee joins an organization, their identity provider, such as an HR system or directory service, can automatically send a SCIM POST request to create the user in all necessary applications. The request includes predefined attributes such as the user's name, email address, department, and role. Once the user record is created, SCIM ensures that this data is synchronized across all connected systems, granting the user access to required services without delays.

Updating user information is another critical aspect of SCIM-based identity management. Employees frequently change roles, departments, or contact details, requiring updates to their identity records. SCIM provides efficient mechanisms for modifying user attributes through PATCH or PUT requests. A PATCH request allows for partial updates, modifying only specific attributes without affecting the rest of the user profile. This approach minimizes unnecessary data transfers and ensures that identity changes are processed in real time. For example, when an employee is promoted to a managerial role, their

SCIM record can be updated to reflect their new title and permissions across all integrated applications.

Deprovisioning users is a vital function in identity management, ensuring that individuals who leave an organization no longer have access to corporate systems. SCIM enables automated deprovisioning through DELETE requests, which remove user accounts from service providers as soon as an individual's employment ends. This reduces the risk of orphaned accounts, which could be exploited by attackers or lead to unauthorized access. Organizations implementing SCIM can enforce strict deactivation policies to maintain security and compliance while streamlining the offboarding process.

Groups in SCIM serve as logical collections of users that share common access permissions, making them an essential tool for managing identity access at scale. A SCIM group consists of a unique identifier, a display name, and a list of member users. Groups simplify access control by allowing administrators to assign permissions at the group level instead of managing access for each user individually. This improves efficiency and ensures that access rights remain consistent across an organization.

Group creation follows a process similar to user creation, with a SCIM POST request defining the group name and its initial members. When an organization creates a new team or department, a corresponding SCIM group can be generated to grant access to shared resources automatically. For example, a company might create groups such as "Finance Team," "Marketing Department," or "Developers," each with predefined access to relevant applications. Once a user is assigned to a SCIM group, they inherit the associated permissions, allowing them to access necessary tools without requiring manual configuration.

Managing group memberships in SCIM is a dynamic process that allows users to be added or removed based on role changes, department transfers, or security policies. When an employee transitions to a new team, a SCIM PATCH request can update their group memberships without requiring individual access modifications. This ensures that users always have the correct permissions based on their current responsibilities. Automatic group membership updates reduce administrative effort and improve security by preventing outdated access assignments.

SCIM also supports dynamic groups, where membership is determined based on predefined criteria rather than manual assignment. Dynamic groups allow organizations to create rules that automatically include users based on attributes such as job title, department, or location. For instance, all employees in the "Sales" department can be automatically assigned to the "Sales Team" group, ensuring that they receive the necessary permissions without requiring manual updates. This approach streamlines identity management and reduces the risk of misconfigured access.

Group deletion in SCIM follows a structured process that removes access privileges from all associated members. When a department is dissolved or a project is completed, its corresponding SCIM group can be deleted using a DELETE request. This ensures that unnecessary groups do not clutter identity management systems and that permissions remain accurate. Removing a group automatically revokes access for all its members, enforcing strict access control policies and reducing the risk of unauthorized resource usage.

SCIM provides efficient mechanisms for querying and retrieving user and group information, enabling organizations to monitor identity records effectively. The SCIM GET request allows identity providers to retrieve a list of all users or groups, filter results based on specific attributes, and sort records for easier management. Large enterprises with thousands of employees benefit from SCIM's pagination and filtering capabilities, which optimize performance by limiting the amount of data returned in a single request. For example, an administrator may retrieve all users within a specific department or identify inactive accounts for review.

Bulk operations in SCIM enhance efficiency by allowing multiple user and group updates to be processed in a single request. This feature is particularly useful for onboarding or offboarding large numbers of employees simultaneously. Instead of sending separate API calls for each user, SCIM enables organizations to create, update, or delete multiple records at once, reducing network overhead and improving response times. Bulk operations ensure consistency and accuracy in identity management, especially in large-scale environments where frequent identity changes occur.

Security considerations in SCIM-based user and group management include authentication, authorization, and access control enforcement. SCIM integrates with authentication standards such as OAuth 2.0 to ensure that only authorized clients can perform identity-related operations. All SCIM communications occur over secure HTTPS connections to prevent data interception. Organizations implementing SCIM must enforce strict access policies to protect user and group data from unauthorized modifications. Maintaining audit logs of SCIM transactions provides visibility into identity changes and supports compliance with security regulations.

The adoption of SCIM for user and group management simplifies identity synchronization across diverse IT environments. By standardizing how users and groups are created, updated, and deprovisioned, SCIM reduces administrative workload and improves security. Automating identity lifecycle management ensures that access permissions remain accurate, minimizing the risks associated with outdated credentials and manual errors. Organizations that implement SCIM benefit from a scalable, consistent, and secure approach to managing user identities and group memberships across their digital ecosystem.

SCIM Schema and Extensions

The System for Cross-domain Identity Management (SCIM) is built on a standardized schema that defines how identity data is structured and exchanged between identity providers and service providers. The SCIM schema ensures that user and group information is represented consistently, reducing integration complexity and promoting interoperability across different identity management systems. By providing a common format for identity attributes, SCIM simplifies provisioning, synchronization, and access control, making identity management more efficient for organizations operating in cloud and hybrid environments.

The SCIM schema is designed to be flexible, allowing organizations to manage a variety of identity-related data while maintaining consistency across different applications. At its core, SCIM defines two primary resources: Users and Groups. The User resource contains standard attributes such as userName, givenName, familyName, email, phoneNumbers, and roles. These attributes form the basis of identity representation in SCIM, ensuring that user records include the essential information needed for authentication and authorization. Each user has a unique identifier (id), which remains constant across updates to ensure consistency in identity synchronization.

The Group resource follows a similar structured schema, defining attributes such as displayName and members. Groups are essential for role-based access control, allowing organizations to assign permissions collectively rather than managing individual user permissions manually. Each group has a unique identifier, and its membership list contains references to user objects, ensuring that group assignments are consistently maintained across identity systems. The SCIM schema for groups makes it easy to manage access control policies dynamically by adding or removing users from groups as needed.

SCIM uses a structured data model based on JSON, making it easy to transmit and process identity information using modern web technologies. Each resource in SCIM follows a predictable format, ensuring that identity providers and service providers can exchange data without ambiguity. The SCIM schema is designed to support both required and optional attributes, allowing for flexibility while maintaining a consistent structure. Mandatory attributes, such as userName for users and displayName for groups, ensure that essential identity information is always included, while optional attributes provide additional details that can be used to enhance identity management processes.

SCIM supports attribute mutability, allowing certain attributes to be modified while keeping others immutable. Some attributes, such as userName and id, are considered immutable and cannot be changed after creation, ensuring identity integrity. Other attributes, such as email, roles, and phoneNumbers, can be updated based on changes in user information. This structured approach ensures that identity updates are handled efficiently and consistently across different systems.

One of the most powerful features of SCIM is its support for extensions, which allow organizations to customize the schema to meet their specific identity management requirements. While the SCIM core schema provides a standardized set of attributes, organizations often need to store additional information that is not covered by the default schema. SCIM extensions provide a way to define custom attributes without disrupting interoperability with standard SCIM implementations.

SCIM extensions are defined using a unique namespace that distinguishes them from the core schema. When an extension is introduced, it follows a structured format that includes additional attributes relevant to a particular use case. For example, an organization managing employee records may extend the SCIM schema to include attributes such as employeeNumber, jobTitle, department, or manager. These attributes provide additional context for identity management while maintaining compatibility with existing SCIM implementations.

Service providers implementing SCIM can define their own extensions to support industry-specific identity attributes. For example, a healthcare organization may extend the SCIM schema to include attributes related to professional certifications, licensing numbers, or medical roles. A financial institution may introduce extensions for regulatory compliance attributes, such as risk classification levels or audit history. These extensions allow SCIM to be adapted for specialized identity management requirements without requiring changes to the core protocol.

SCIM also supports enterprise user extensions, which are commonly used by organizations to enhance user identity records. The enterprise user extension, defined under the namespace urn:ietf:params:scim:schemas:extension:enterprise:2.0:User, includes attributes such as employeeNumber, costCenter, organization, division, department, manager, and managerId. These attributes help organizations manage workforce identity information more effectively, ensuring that user records include relevant employment details.

When implementing SCIM extensions, organizations must ensure that custom attributes follow a structured and consistent format.

Extensions should be clearly documented, specifying attribute data types, required fields, and validation rules. Maintaining proper documentation helps prevent interoperability issues when integrating SCIM with multiple identity providers and service providers. SCIM consumers must be designed to handle both standard and extended attributes gracefully, ensuring that identity synchronization processes remain reliable even when custom attributes are introduced.

SCIM allows identity providers to retrieve schema definitions dynamically, enabling clients to discover supported attributes and extensions programmatically. The Schema resource in SCIM provides a way for clients to query the supported attributes for users, groups, and any extensions implemented by a service provider. This ensures that identity providers can adapt to different SCIM implementations without requiring manual configuration. By querying the schema dynamically, organizations can verify attribute compatibility before exchanging identity data, improving integration reliability.

The Service Provider Configuration resource in SCIM further enhances schema management by providing metadata about the supported SCIM implementation. This resource includes details about supported authentication methods, schema extensions, and API capabilities. Identity providers can use this information to ensure that their SCIM integration aligns with the features available in a given SCIM implementation. By defining service provider capabilities clearly, SCIM reduces integration complexity and promotes seamless identity synchronization.

SCIM schema validation ensures that identity data remains structured and consistent. When a SCIM request is processed, service providers enforce attribute validation rules to prevent malformed data from being stored. Attributes must conform to the expected data types, character limits, and formatting conventions specified in the schema definition. Schema validation helps maintain data integrity and prevents errors that could disrupt identity synchronization processes.

SCIM's schema and extension capabilities make it a versatile and adaptable framework for managing identities across diverse environments. By providing a standardized structure for user and group attributes, SCIM simplifies identity provisioning, access management, and synchronization between identity providers and service providers. The ability to extend the schema ensures that SCIM can accommodate industry-specific requirements while maintaining interoperability with standard implementations. Organizations leveraging SCIM for identity management benefit from a flexible and scalable solution that integrates seamlessly with modern cloud-based and enterprise identity systems.

Authentication and Authorization in SCIM

Authentication and authorization are critical components of SCIM, ensuring that only authorized entities can access and modify identity data. As SCIM is designed to facilitate identity provisioning and synchronization across different systems, securing access to SCIM endpoints is essential to protect user and group data from unauthorized changes, data breaches, and other security threats. SCIM relies on modern authentication and authorization protocols, including OAuth 2.0, bearer tokens, and client credentials, to enforce strict access control policies while enabling seamless integration between identity providers and service providers.

Authentication in SCIM ensures that clients making requests to SCIM endpoints are verified before they can retrieve, create, update, or delete identity data. One of the most common authentication mechanisms used in SCIM implementations is OAuth 2.0, a widely adopted protocol for securing API access. OAuth 2.0 provides a flexible and secure way to authenticate clients while minimizing the risks associated with handling sensitive credentials directly. By using OAuth tokens, SCIM services can enforce authentication without requiring clients to repeatedly send passwords or API keys in their requests.

OAuth 2.0 supports different grant types, depending on the use case and the level of security required. The client credentials grant is commonly used for SCIM integrations, where an identity provider and a service provider establish a trusted relationship. In this scenario, the client application authenticates using a client ID and client secret, which are exchanged for an access token. This token is then included in SCIM API requests as a bearer token in the HTTP authorization header. By using token-based authentication, SCIM ensures that credentials are not exposed in every request, reducing the risk of interception and credential theft.

Service providers implementing SCIM may also support basic authentication using HTTP headers with usernames and passwords. While this method is simpler to implement, it is considered less secure than OAuth 2.0, as credentials must be transmitted in every request. When basic authentication is used, SCIM services must enforce HTTPS encryption to prevent credentials from being intercepted in transit. To enhance security, many SCIM implementations disable basic authentication in favor of token-based authentication mechanisms.

Authorization in SCIM determines what actions a client is allowed to perform on SCIM resources. While authentication verifies the identity of the client, authorization defines the level of access granted to the client based on roles, policies, and permissions. SCIM enforces authorization by implementing role-based access control (RBAC) and attribute-based access control (ABAC), ensuring that only authorized clients can modify user and group data.

RBAC in SCIM assigns permissions based on predefined roles, ensuring that users and applications have access only to the resources they are authorized to manage. For example, an administrator role may have full access to create, update, and delete SCIM users and groups, while a read-only role may only have permission to retrieve identity data without making modifications. By defining clear role-based policies, SCIM reduces the risk of unauthorized access and accidental data modifications.

ABAC extends authorization by evaluating specific attributes when determining access permissions. Instead of relying solely on predefined roles, ABAC considers contextual attributes such as user department, location, authentication method, or time of access. This approach allows organizations to implement more granular access controls, ensuring that SCIM operations align with security policies and compliance requirements. For example, an ABAC policy could restrict identity modifications to users who authenticate from a corporate network while allowing read access from external locations.

SCIM also supports fine-grained authorization policies by restricting access to specific attributes within user and group objects. In some scenarios, certain attributes, such as email addresses or role assignments, may require higher privileges to modify. By enforcing attribute-level authorization, SCIM ensures that sensitive identity attributes are protected and only modified by authorized clients. This prevents unintended changes to critical identity data while allowing lower-privileged clients to access non-sensitive attributes.

Access tokens used in SCIM authentication and authorization often have expiration times, ensuring that credentials are not valid indefinitely. When a token expires, the client must request a new token before continuing to interact with the SCIM API. This approach limits the risk associated with compromised tokens, as attackers cannot reuse expired credentials to gain unauthorized access. Refresh tokens can be implemented to allow clients to obtain new access tokens without requiring reauthentication, improving both security and usability.

Logging and auditing are essential components of SCIM security, providing visibility into authentication and authorization events. SCIM services typically maintain detailed logs of authentication attempts, token issuance, and API requests to detect suspicious activity. By analyzing these logs, organizations can identify potential security threats, such as repeated failed authentication attempts or unauthorized access attempts. Audit logs also support compliance with security regulations, providing a record of identity-related changes for review and reporting purposes.

SCIM implementations must enforce best practices for securing authentication credentials and access tokens. Clients should store secrets securely, avoiding hardcoded credentials in application code. Tokens should be stored in a secure vault or encrypted storage to prevent unauthorized access. When using OAuth 2.0, SCIM services should follow recommended security practices, such as enforcing token scopes, limiting token lifetimes, and requiring multi-factor authentication (MFA) for high-privilege operations.

Identity federation plays an important role in SCIM authentication and authorization, allowing organizations to leverage existing identity providers to manage access control. SCIM can integrate with identity federation protocols such as OpenID Connect and SAML to extend authentication capabilities beyond direct API interactions. By federating authentication, SCIM services can rely on trusted identity providers to verify users and issue access tokens, reducing the need for separate authentication mechanisms.

SCIM's authentication and authorization mechanisms ensure that identity data remains protected while allowing seamless identity synchronization across applications and services. By enforcing strong authentication methods such as OAuth 2.0 and implementing role-based and attribute-based access controls, SCIM minimizes security risks while maintaining flexibility in managing user and group data. Organizations implementing SCIM must follow security best practices to ensure that identity operations are securely executed, reducing the risk of unauthorized access and identity-related attacks.

Implementing a SCIM Provider

Implementing a SCIM provider requires designing and deploying a system that can manage user and group identities in compliance with the SCIM protocol. A SCIM provider acts as the authoritative source of identity data, exposing a RESTful API that allows identity consumers, such as service providers, to create, update, retrieve, and delete users and groups. The implementation of a SCIM provider must align with the SCIM 2.0 specification, ensuring interoperability with different identity management systems and applications.

The first step in implementing a SCIM provider is defining the SCIM endpoints that will be exposed. The SCIM protocol follows a REST-based architecture, requiring the provider to implement standard HTTP methods such as GET, POST, PUT, PATCH, and DELETE. Each SCIM resource, including users and groups, has a corresponding endpoint where identity operations are performed. The provider must correctly handle API requests at these endpoints, ensuring compliance with SCIM data structures and response formats.

The user resource is one of the most critical components of a SCIM provider. Each user object follows the SCIM schema, containing attributes such as userName, givenName, familyName, email, and phoneNumbers. The provider must implement logic to store and retrieve these attributes, ensuring that user data is structured according to SCIM standards. When a service provider sends a POST request to create a new user, the SCIM provider must validate the request, generate a unique user identifier, and store the user record in its identity database. The response must include the newly created user object with all required attributes populated.

Updating user data is another key function of a SCIM provider. Identity information frequently changes as users update their personal details, change roles, or transition between departments. The SCIM provider must support both full and partial updates using PUT and PATCH requests. A PUT request replaces the entire user object with new data, while a PATCH request modifies only the specified attributes. Proper validation and error handling are necessary to ensure that only allowed attributes are modified, preventing unintended data corruption.

The deletion of users must be handled securely and efficiently. When a DELETE request is received for a user, the SCIM provider must determine whether to perform a hard delete, removing the user from the system entirely, or a soft delete, marking the user as inactive while retaining their data for compliance purposes. Organizations implementing SCIM often prefer soft deletes to allow for user account restoration if needed. The SCIM provider must enforce proper access controls to prevent unauthorized deletions and ensure that deactivated users cannot access services.

Managing group identities is another essential function of a SCIM provider. Groups are collections of users with shared permissions, used to simplify access control in enterprise environments. The SCIM provider must implement endpoints for creating, updating, retrieving, and deleting groups, ensuring that group membership remains consistent. When a service provider sends a POST request to create a group, the SCIM provider must validate the request, generate a unique group identifier, and store the group object in its identity database. The response must include the group details along with a list of its members.

Group membership management requires supporting operations to add or remove users from groups dynamically. When a user is added to a SCIM group, the provider must update the group object and synchronize the change across connected applications. Similarly, when a user is removed from a group, the provider must ensure that their access permissions are revoked accordingly. Proper auditing of group membership changes is necessary to maintain compliance with security policies and prevent unauthorized access.

Authentication and authorization play a crucial role in securing a SCIM provider. To prevent unauthorized access to identity data, the SCIM provider must implement secure authentication mechanisms such as OAuth 2.0. Clients interacting with the SCIM provider must present valid access tokens to authenticate API requests. These tokens should be validated before processing any SCIM operation, ensuring that only authorized clients can manage identities. The provider must also enforce role-based access controls (RBAC) to restrict which operations different clients can perform. For example, an administrator may have full access to user and group management, while a read-only client may only retrieve identity records.

Performance and scalability considerations must be addressed when implementing a SCIM provider. Large enterprises manage thousands or even millions of user identities, requiring efficient handling of SCIM requests. The provider must support pagination, filtering, and sorting to optimize data retrieval. Pagination ensures that responses are limited to a manageable number of records per request, reducing server load and improving API performance. Filtering allows clients to request only relevant user records based on specific attributes, such as department or role. Sorting enables results to be ordered based on predefined criteria, enhancing usability for identity management applications.

Bulk operations are an important feature that a SCIM provider must support to improve efficiency. Instead of processing individual SCIM requests for each user or group modification, the provider should implement a bulk API that allows multiple operations to be executed in a single request. Bulk operations reduce network overhead and enhance performance during large-scale identity updates, such as employee onboarding, offboarding, or access revocation. Proper error handling must be implemented to ensure that failures in individual operations do not disrupt the entire bulk request.

Logging and auditing are essential components of a SCIM provider, ensuring visibility into identity changes and API interactions. The provider must maintain detailed logs of all SCIM requests, including authentication attempts, user modifications, group membership changes, and failed requests. These logs help organizations detect security incidents, troubleshoot identity synchronization issues, and comply with regulatory requirements. Audit logs should be protected against tampering and stored securely for compliance and forensic analysis.

Schema extensibility is another consideration when implementing a SCIM provider. While SCIM defines a core schema for users and groups, organizations may need to extend the schema to accommodate additional attributes. The provider must support custom extensions while maintaining compatibility with standard SCIM attributes. Proper documentation of schema extensions ensures that service providers interacting with the SCIM API can understand and utilize the additional attributes correctly.

Error handling is a critical aspect of a SCIM provider implementation. When processing SCIM requests, the provider must return appropriate HTTP status codes and descriptive error messages. A 400 Bad Request response should be returned for invalid input data, a 401 Unauthorized response for authentication failures, and a 403 Forbidden response for unauthorized actions. Providing meaningful error messages helps clients diagnose and resolve integration issues more efficiently.

The successful implementation of a SCIM provider requires careful planning and adherence to SCIM standards. By implementing secure authentication, efficient user and group management, proper access controls, and scalable performance optimizations, organizations can build a robust SCIM provider that streamlines identity provisioning and synchronization.

Implementing a SCIM Consumer

Implementing a SCIM consumer involves designing a system that can connect to a SCIM provider, retrieve user and group data, and process identity updates efficiently. A SCIM consumer is typically a service provider or application that requires identity data to manage user authentication, authorization, and access control. By consuming SCIM endpoints, the system can automate user provisioning, synchronize identity attributes, and ensure that access permissions remain up to date across different platforms. A well-implemented SCIM consumer follows the SCIM 2.0 specification, ensuring compatibility with identity providers while handling identity changes in a secure and scalable manner.

The first step in implementing a SCIM consumer is establishing a connection to a SCIM provider. The consumer must authenticate using a supported method, such as OAuth 2.0, to obtain an access token before making API requests. Authentication ensures that only authorized clients can interact with the SCIM provider, preventing unauthorized access to identity data. The consumer must handle token expiration by refreshing or requesting a new token when needed, ensuring continuous access without interruptions. Proper handling of authentication failures is critical to maintaining a reliable identity synchronization process.

Retrieving user data is one of the primary functions of a SCIM consumer. When a user is created or modified in the identity provider, the consumer must fetch the latest user attributes to reflect these changes in its system. The consumer sends a GET request to the SCIM /Users endpoint to retrieve user records, specifying filters if necessary to limit the results. The response includes user details such as userName, givenName, familyName, email, phoneNumbers, and any additional attributes defined in the SCIM schema. The consumer must parse the response and update its internal user records accordingly.

User synchronization can be handled in two ways: periodic polling or event-driven updates. In periodic polling, the consumer regularly queries the SCIM provider to check for changes, ensuring that user data remains consistent. This approach requires careful tuning of polling intervals to balance performance and data freshness. In an event-driven model, the SCIM provider notifies the consumer of identity changes using a webhook or push notification mechanism. This approach reduces API load and ensures that updates are processed in real time, making it more efficient for large-scale identity management.

Handling user updates requires the SCIM consumer to track changes in identity attributes and apply them appropriately. When a user updates their email, phone number, or role in the identity provider, the consumer must fetch the modified attributes and synchronize them with its internal records. Partial updates can be processed using PATCH requests, which modify only the affected attributes rather than replacing the entire user object. Proper logging and auditing of user updates help detect synchronization issues and ensure compliance with security policies.

Deprovisioning users is a critical function that ensures former employees or unauthorized users do not retain access to applications. When a SCIM provider marks a user as inactive or deletes their record, the consumer must detect this change and revoke the user's access. A DELETE request from the provider indicates that the user should be removed, while a status change in the user record may require suspending the account instead of immediate deletion. Handling deprovisioning properly reduces security risks associated with orphaned accounts and ensures compliance with access control policies.

Group synchronization is another key aspect of SCIM consumer implementation. Groups define collections of users who share common access permissions, simplifying role-based access control (RBAC) in applications. The consumer retrieves group data by sending a GET request to the SCIM /Groups endpoint, fetching details such as displayName and members. When a user is added to or removed from a SCIM group, the consumer must update its internal role assignments accordingly. This ensures that users automatically receive or lose access to features based on their group memberships.

Managing dynamic and static groups requires careful handling in a SCIM consumer. Static groups have explicitly assigned members, while dynamic groups determine membership based on attributes such as department or job title. When processing dynamic group assignments, the consumer must evaluate attribute conditions and update user memberships accordingly. Any changes in user attributes that affect dynamic group membership must trigger access updates to maintain consistency in permissions.

Performance optimization is essential when implementing a SCIM consumer, particularly when dealing with large identity datasets. Filtering, pagination, and sorting help improve efficiency when retrieving user and group data. Instead of fetching all records at once, the consumer can use pagination to retrieve a limited number of records per request, reducing network overhead. Filtering allows selective retrieval of users based on criteria such as department, role, or status, minimizing unnecessary data processing. Sorting ensures that results are returned in a structured manner, improving data management workflows.

Error handling is a critical component of a SCIM consumer implementation. When interacting with a SCIM provider, the consumer must handle API failures, such as network timeouts, authentication errors, and malformed responses. HTTP status codes provide valuable insights into request outcomes. A 400 Bad Request indicates an issue with the request format, a 401 Unauthorized suggests an authentication failure, and a 403 Forbidden means the client lacks the necessary permissions. The consumer must implement retry mechanisms for transient errors and log failed requests for troubleshooting.

Security best practices must be followed to protect identity data in a SCIM consumer. All API requests must be transmitted over HTTPS to prevent data interception. Sensitive information such as access tokens and user credentials must be stored securely and never exposed in logs or application configurations. Role-based access controls should be enforced within the consumer application to prevent unauthorized modifications to synchronized identity data. Audit logs should capture all identity synchronization events, helping organizations track changes and investigate security incidents.

Schema handling is another important consideration for SCIM consumers. While SCIM defines a standard schema for users and groups, different providers may implement schema extensions with additional attributes. The consumer must be designed to process these extensions without breaking compatibility with standard SCIM attributes. Querying the SCIM /Schemas endpoint allows the consumer to discover supported attributes dynamically and adjust its data processing logic accordingly. By maintaining flexibility in schema handling, the consumer can integrate with a variety of SCIM providers while supporting custom identity attributes.

Testing and validation are essential before deploying a SCIM consumer in a production environment. The consumer should be tested against multiple SCIM providers to verify interoperability and identify potential compatibility issues. Edge cases such as partial updates, bulk operations, and network failures must be thoroughly tested to ensure resilience. Performance benchmarks should be conducted to evaluate how the consumer handles large-scale identity synchronization and high API request loads. Logging and monitoring should be enabled to track API interactions and detect anomalies in synchronization behavior.

A well-implemented SCIM consumer ensures seamless integration with identity providers, automating user and group synchronization while maintaining security and performance. By adhering to SCIM standards and best practices, organizations can reduce administrative overhead, enhance access control, and improve identity management across their applications and services.

SCIM Endpoints and HTTP Methods

SCIM operates through a well-defined set of endpoints and HTTP methods that enable identity management operations such as user and group provisioning, updates, retrieval, and deletion. These endpoints serve as the access points for SCIM clients, allowing them to interact with SCIM providers in a standardized manner. By following RESTful principles, SCIM ensures that identity-related actions can be performed efficiently across different systems while maintaining compatibility with various identity management platforms. The structured use of HTTP methods aligns with modern API best practices, making SCIM a reliable solution for automating identity synchronization.

The core SCIM endpoints revolve around managing users and groups, which are the primary resources in the SCIM protocol. The /Users endpoint is used to create, retrieve, update, and delete user records. Each user is uniquely identified by an id attribute, ensuring consistency across different systems. When a client wants to retrieve all users, it sends a GET request to /Users, and the SCIM provider responds with a paginated list of user objects. If a specific user needs to be retrieved, the request includes the user's unique identifier, such as /Users/{id}, allowing the client to fetch detailed information about a single user.

Creating a new user in SCIM requires sending a POST request to the /Users endpoint with a JSON payload containing the user's attributes. This request must follow the SCIM schema, including required fields such as userName, emails, and name. Upon successful creation, the SCIM provider responds with a 201 Created status and returns the newly created user object, including the assigned id. If any required attributes are missing or formatted incorrectly, the provider responds with a 400 Bad Request error, prompting the client to correct the request.

Updating user attributes is accomplished through PUT or PATCH requests. A PUT request is used when replacing the entire user object with new data, ensuring that all attributes are updated to match the request payload. If a client wishes to modify only specific attributes, a PATCH request is preferred, as it allows partial updates without overwriting unchanged fields. The PATCH request includes an operations array that specifies which attributes should be added, replaced, or removed. For example, if an email address needs to be updated, the PATCH request includes an operation targeting the emails attribute, modifying only that field while leaving other attributes unchanged.

Deleting a user is performed using a DELETE request to the /Users/{id} endpoint. This operation removes the user from the SCIM provider, revoking their access across all connected services. Some SCIM implementations support soft deletes, where the user record is marked as inactive instead of being permanently removed. The provider may return a 204 No Content response to indicate that the deletion was successful. If the user does not exist, a 404 Not Found error is returned, signaling that the requested resource is not available.

The /Groups endpoint functions similarly to /Users, enabling the management of user groups. A GET request to /Groups retrieves a list of all groups, while a GET request to /Groups/{id} fetches details about a specific group. Creating a new group requires a POST request to

/Groups, including attributes such as displayName and members. The members attribute contains a list of user references, allowing SCIM clients to define group memberships when creating the group. The response to a successful POST request includes the group object along with its assigned id.

Updating group memberships follows the same principles as user updates, using either PUT or PATCH requests. A PUT request replaces the entire group object, requiring all members to be specified in the request. If only certain users need to be added or removed, a PATCH request is more efficient, as it modifies only the affected attributes. For example, a PATCH request can add a new user to a group by including an operation that appends a user reference to the members array. Removing a user from a group requires another PATCH operation, specifying the user reference to be deleted.

Deleting a group is performed using a DELETE request to /Groups/{id}, which removes the group from the SCIM provider. This operation may also trigger the revocation of access for all group members, depending on how permissions are enforced within the organization. If the group is already deleted or does not exist, the provider returns a 404 Not Found error.

SCIM also provides additional endpoints for retrieving metadata about the provider's capabilities. The /ServiceProviderConfig endpoint returns information about supported authentication methods, schema versions, and feature support. Clients can send a GET request to /ServiceProviderConfig to determine whether the SCIM provider supports filtering, pagination, and sorting. This allows clients to adapt their requests based on the provider's capabilities, ensuring compatibility with different SCIM implementations.

The /Schemas endpoint provides details about the SCIM schema, including the attributes available for users, groups, and any custom extensions. A GET request to /Schemas returns a list of all supported schemas, allowing clients to dynamically discover attribute definitions. This is particularly useful when integrating with SCIM providers that implement custom extensions, as clients can retrieve schema information programmatically instead of relying on static documentation.

The /ResourceTypes endpoint offers insight into the types of resources available in the SCIM provider. A GET request to /ResourceTypes returns a list of supported resource categories, such as users, groups, and custom objects. This endpoint helps SCIM clients understand the data model of the provider, ensuring that requests align with the available resources.

SCIM also supports bulk operations through the /Bulk endpoint, which allows multiple create, update, and delete operations to be processed in a single request. A POST request to /Bulk includes an array of SCIM operations, each specifying the target resource and the action to be performed. Bulk operations improve efficiency when managing large numbers of users or groups, reducing the number of API calls needed for provisioning and synchronization. The response to a bulk request includes individual status codes for each operation, allowing clients to handle errors and partial successes appropriately.

The combination of SCIM endpoints and HTTP methods provides a robust framework for identity management, enabling seamless integration between identity providers and service providers. By following standardized API interactions, SCIM ensures that user and group data can be managed consistently across different systems. The structured use of GET, POST, PUT, PATCH, and DELETE methods allows for efficient identity synchronization while maintaining security and data integrity. Proper implementation of SCIM endpoints enables organizations to automate identity provisioning, streamline access control, and maintain compliance with identity governance policies.

SCIM Attributes and Mapping

SCIM defines a standardized way to manage identity information across different systems, ensuring interoperability between identity providers and service providers. At the core of SCIM's functionality is its attribute model, which specifies the data elements that describe users, groups, and other identity-related entities. Proper attribute mapping between SCIM and external identity systems is essential for accurate provisioning, synchronization, and deprovisioning. By following a structured approach to attribute management, organizations can maintain data consistency, improve access control, and reduce manual administrative efforts.

SCIM attributes are organized within a defined schema, which provides a consistent structure for identity information. The User resource includes attributes such as userName, givenName, familyName, emails, phoneNumbers, roles, and active. These attributes represent fundamental identity details required for authentication, communication, and access management. Each user is assigned a globally unique id, ensuring that identity records remain consistent even when attributes are updated.

The Group resource contains attributes such as displayName, members, and id. Groups allow for collective identity management, enabling administrators to assign permissions and roles at a group level rather than individually configuring user access. The members attribute consists of a list of user references, defining which individuals belong to a specific group. The structured representation of groups simplifies role-based access control, ensuring that users receive the appropriate permissions based on their assignments.

Each SCIM attribute follows a specific data type and structure. Attributes can be simple types such as strings, numbers, and booleans, or they can be complex objects containing nested attributes. For example, the emails attribute is a multi-valued complex type that includes fields for value, type, and primary. This structure allows users to have multiple email addresses categorized as work, home, or other types. Similarly, the phoneNumbers attribute follows a similar pattern, enabling multiple phone numbers to be stored with corresponding labels.

Attribute mutability defines how SCIM attributes can be modified. Some attributes are immutable, meaning they cannot be changed once set. The id attribute, for instance, remains constant throughout the user's lifecycle to maintain identity consistency. Other attributes, such as givenName and familyName, are read-write, allowing updates when a user's personal details change. Attributes like meta.created and meta.lastModified are read-only, as they are automatically managed by the SCIM provider. Understanding mutability is crucial when mapping attributes between SCIM and external systems to prevent unintended modifications.

Mapping SCIM attributes to external identity systems is a key step in integrating SCIM with directory services, cloud applications, and custom identity platforms. Many organizations rely on LDAP directories, Active Directory, or cloud-based identity providers such as Microsoft Entra ID, Okta, and Google Workspace. To ensure proper identity synchronization, SCIM attributes must be mapped to their corresponding fields in these systems. For example, the SCIM userName attribute is often mapped to sAMAccountName in Active Directory or uid in LDAP. Similarly, the SCIM emails.value attribute may correspond to mail in LDAP or emailAddress in a cloud identity platform.

Handling attribute transformations is sometimes necessary when mapping SCIM attributes to external systems. Different platforms may store data in varying formats, requiring modifications to ensure compatibility. For instance, some directories store phone numbers in a raw numeric format, while SCIM expects them to be structured with type labels. In such cases, transformation rules can be applied to convert attribute values into the required format. When mapping attributes such as displayName, which may be constructed from givenName and familyName, concatenation logic is applied to generate a properly formatted value.

Multi-valued attributes require special handling when performing attribute mapping. SCIM allows certain attributes, such as emails and phoneNumbers, to contain multiple values, whereas some external systems only support single-valued fields. To resolve this discrepancy, organizations must decide whether to store only the primary value, concatenate multiple values, or use an alternate storage method to preserve additional values. When integrating with systems that do not support multi-valued attributes, careful planning is required to prevent data loss or inconsistencies.

Custom attributes can be introduced when organizations require additional identity fields beyond the SCIM core schema. SCIM provides an extension mechanism that allows organizations to define custom attributes under a unique namespace. These extensions ensure that custom fields can be added without breaking compatibility with standard SCIM implementations. For example, an enterprise may introduce attributes such as employeeNumber, costCenter, or managerId to track internal HR and organizational data. The ability to extend the SCIM schema allows businesses to tailor identity management to their specific needs while maintaining interoperability.

Ensuring attribute consistency across different systems is a challenge when integrating SCIM. Identity data may originate from multiple sources, including HR systems, directory services, and authentication providers. Synchronization rules must be established to determine which system serves as the authoritative source for specific attributes. For example, HR systems may be the source of truth for attributes such as givenName, familyName, and jobTitle, while authentication systems manage password and multi-factor authentication settings. Defining clear ownership rules prevents conflicts and ensures that attribute updates are correctly propagated.

Handling attribute conflicts is essential when multiple systems modify the same identity attributes. When a user updates their profile information in one system, the changes must be reconciled with other connected platforms. Conflict resolution strategies include prioritizing updates based on source system trust levels, using timestamps to determine the most recent changes, or implementing manual review processes for critical attribute modifications. SCIM providers must implement versioning and audit logs to track attribute changes, providing visibility into identity updates and helping administrators resolve conflicts when necessary.

Security and privacy considerations must be taken into account when mapping SCIM attributes. Some attributes, such as password, socialSecurityNumber, and biometricData, contain sensitive information that requires additional protection. Organizations must enforce access controls to ensure that only authorized clients can retrieve or modify specific attributes. SCIM supports attribute filtering, allowing service providers to restrict which attributes are exposed to different clients based on permission levels. Encryption and hashing techniques should be applied to sensitive attributes to enhance security and protect user data from unauthorized access.

Auditing and logging attribute changes is an important aspect of maintaining identity data integrity. SCIM providers should generate logs that track when attributes are modified, who made the changes, and what values were updated. These logs help organizations monitor identity synchronization, detect anomalies, and comply with regulatory requirements. By maintaining an audit trail of attribute changes, organizations can identify potential security incidents and ensure that identity data remains accurate across all connected systems.

A well-structured approach to SCIM attribute management and mapping ensures that identity data remains consistent, accurate, and secure. Proper alignment of SCIM attributes with external identity systems enables seamless user provisioning, access control enforcement, and automated identity synchronization. By understanding SCIM's attribute model, handling data transformations, and implementing security best practices, organizations can optimize identity management and maintain compliance across their digital environments.

Handling SCIM Bulk Operations

SCIM provides a standardized approach for managing identity data across different systems, ensuring efficient user provisioning, synchronization, and access control. One of the key features of SCIM is its support for bulk operations, which allow multiple identity management tasks to be performed in a single request. Bulk operations help reduce network overhead, improve performance, and streamline identity updates, making them essential for large-scale identity management scenarios. By handling multiple create, update, or delete operations at once, organizations can efficiently manage thousands of users and groups while maintaining consistency across identity systems.

The SCIM bulk operations endpoint allows clients to send a single request containing multiple operations, each specifying the action to be performed on a user or group. Instead of making individual API calls for each operation, a bulk request consolidates them into a single transaction, reducing the number of round trips between the SCIM client and provider. This approach minimizes latency, improves API efficiency, and ensures that identity modifications are processed together, reducing the risk of partial failures or inconsistencies.

A SCIM bulk request is structured as a JSON object containing an array of operations. Each operation includes details such as the HTTP method (POST, PUT, PATCH, or DELETE), the target resource (Users or Groups), and the data required to perform the action. When processing a bulk request, the SCIM provider executes each operation in sequence, applying changes to identity records and returning individual responses for each action. This structure allows clients to track which operations succeeded, which failed, and any error messages that may have occurred.

Bulk user creation is one of the most common use cases for SCIM bulk operations. When an organization hires a large number of employees, their user accounts must be provisioned in multiple applications simultaneously. Instead of sending separate POST requests for each user, a bulk request can include multiple user objects, each with attributes such as userName, emails, name, and roles. The SCIM provider processes these records in a single batch, creating user accounts efficiently and returning the corresponding user IDs in the response. This method significantly reduces the time required for onboarding and ensures that all users are created consistently.

Updating multiple users at once is another key advantage of SCIM bulk operations. Organizations frequently need to modify attributes such as department assignments, job titles, or access permissions for large groups of users. A bulk request containing PATCH operations can update multiple user records in a single transaction, reducing the need for repetitive API calls. Each PATCH operation specifies the attributes to be modified, ensuring that only relevant changes are applied without affecting other user attributes. Bulk updates improve performance and ensure that identity data remains synchronized across connected systems.

Bulk user deletion is critical when employees leave an organization or access to specific applications needs to be revoked. Instead of issuing separate DELETE requests for each user, a bulk request can remove multiple users in one operation. The SCIM provider processes the request by deactivating or permanently deleting the specified user records, ensuring that former employees no longer have access to corporate resources. Bulk deletion reduces the administrative burden on IT teams and improves security by minimizing the risk of orphaned accounts remaining active.

Handling bulk group operations is equally important for efficient identity management. Organizations often need to create or modify multiple groups simultaneously, assigning users to different roles or teams. A bulk request containing POST operations can create several groups at once, each with attributes such as displayName and members. Similarly, PATCH operations allow administrators to update group memberships dynamically, adding or removing users based on changing business requirements. Bulk group updates ensure that access control policies remain aligned with organizational changes, preventing unauthorized access while simplifying administrative tasks.

SCIM bulk operations must be processed carefully to maintain data integrity and ensure that identity changes are applied correctly. The SCIM provider must execute each operation in the order specified by the request, handling dependencies between actions when necessary. For example, if a bulk request includes a user creation followed by adding the user to a group, the provider must ensure that the user record is created before processing the group membership update. Proper sequencing of operations prevents errors and ensures that identity modifications are applied in the correct order.

Error handling in SCIM bulk operations is essential for diagnosing and resolving issues that may arise during processing. If an individual operation within a bulk request fails, the SCIM provider must return a detailed error message indicating the reason for the failure. The response includes an array of results, each containing a status code and an error description for the corresponding operation. Clients can use this information to retry failed operations, correct invalid data, or adjust request formatting as needed. Ensuring clear and informative error messages helps streamline troubleshooting and improves the reliability of SCIM integrations.

Performance optimization is a key consideration when handling SCIM bulk operations, particularly in large-scale environments where thousands of identity records are processed simultaneously. The SCIM provider must implement efficient database transactions, indexing, and caching mechanisms to handle bulk requests without degrading performance. Rate limiting may be enforced to prevent excessive load on the API, ensuring that bulk operations do not impact system stability. Organizations should also define appropriate batch sizes for bulk requests, balancing efficiency with API processing limits to avoid timeouts or resource constraints.

Security considerations must be addressed when processing SCIM bulk operations, as they involve modifying multiple identity records in a single transaction. Authentication and authorization mechanisms must be enforced to ensure that only authorized clients can execute bulk requests. Role-based access controls (RBAC) should restrict bulk operations to privileged administrators, preventing unauthorized modifications to identity data. Logging and auditing mechanisms should capture all bulk operations, providing visibility into identity changes and supporting compliance with security regulations.

SCIM bulk operations enable organizations to manage identity data at scale, improving efficiency, reducing administrative overhead, and ensuring consistency across applications. By leveraging bulk requests for user provisioning, updates, and deprovisioning, organizations can streamline identity synchronization while maintaining security and data integrity. Proper implementation of SCIM bulk operations enhances the scalability of identity management solutions, making them well-suited for enterprise environments with complex identity requirements.

Filtering, Paging, and Sorting in SCIM

SCIM provides mechanisms for efficiently retrieving identity data by supporting filtering, paging, and sorting operations. These features ensure that SCIM clients can request only relevant identity records, optimize API performance, and handle large datasets effectively. By implementing these capabilities, SCIM providers improve the scalability of identity synchronization while reducing unnecessary data transfer between identity providers and service providers.

Filtering allows SCIM clients to retrieve specific user or group records that meet defined criteria. Instead of returning all users or groups in a system, filtering enables clients to request only those that match certain attributes. This improves performance by limiting the amount of data processed and transferred, reducing network load and response times. SCIM filters use logical expressions to compare attribute values, providing flexibility in how identity records are queried.

The SCIM filtering syntax follows a structured format that specifies the attribute name, an operator, and a value. The most commonly used operators include eq (equals), ne (not equal), co (contains), sw (starts with), gt (greater than), and lt (less than). For example, to retrieve all users in the IT department, a SCIM client can send a GET request to /Users?filter=department eq "IT". This request instructs the SCIM provider to return only users whose department attribute is equal to "IT".

Complex filters can be constructed using logical operators such as and and or. These operators allow clients to refine their queries further by combining multiple conditions. For instance, a SCIM client may request users who belong to the IT department and have an active status by sending /Users?filter=department eq "IT" and active eq true. This ensures that only currently active IT employees are returned, making identity management operations more precise and efficient.

Filtering can also be applied to group memberships. A SCIM client can request all groups that contain a specific user by sending /Groups?filter=members eq "user123". This query retrieves only the groups where the user with the identifier user123 is a member, enabling applications to determine a user's access rights based on their group affiliations. Similarly, a client can request all users who belong to a particular group using /Users?filter=groups eq "admin-group".

SCIM filtering is case-sensitive by default, but implementations may allow for case-insensitive comparisons. Some SCIM providers extend filtering capabilities with additional operators or wildcard support, providing even more flexibility in querying identity records. Clients should refer to the /ServiceProviderConfig endpoint to determine the filtering capabilities of a specific SCIM implementation.

Paging is another essential feature in SCIM, designed to handle large datasets by breaking responses into smaller, manageable chunks. When retrieving users or groups, a SCIM provider may store thousands or millions of records. Without paging, a request for all users could result in an overwhelming amount of data being transmitted, leading to performance degradation and potential API timeouts. SCIM solves this issue by allowing clients to specify a start index and a page size, ensuring that responses are limited to a reasonable number of records per request.

The startIndex parameter defines where the returned records should begin, while the count parameter specifies how many records should be included in the response. For example, to retrieve the first 50 users, a SCIM client sends a GET request to /Users?startIndex=1&count=50. The response includes only the first 50 users, along with metadata indicating the total number of users available.

To fetch the next set of users, the client increments the startIndex value while keeping count the same. A request for the second page of results would be /Users?startIndex=51&count=50. This pagination mechanism ensures that large datasets are retrieved in a controlled manner, preventing excessive memory consumption and improving API responsiveness.

SCIM providers include pagination metadata in responses to help clients navigate through multiple pages of results. The response typically contains attributes such as totalResults, startIndex, and itemsPerPage, allowing clients to determine whether additional pages exist. Clients can use this metadata to dynamically adjust pagination logic based on the total number of records available.

Sorting enhances SCIM queries by allowing clients to define the order in which results are returned. Without sorting, SCIM providers may return records in an arbitrary order, making it difficult for clients to process data efficiently. Sorting ensures that results are structured based on specified attributes, improving data retrieval and presentation.

SCIM sorting is controlled using the sortBy and sortOrder parameters. The sortBy parameter specifies the attribute used for sorting, while the sortOrder parameter defines whether results should be sorted in ascending (ascending) or descending (descending) order. For example, to retrieve users sorted by their last names in ascending order, a SCIM client sends /Users?sortBy=familyName&sortOrder=ascending. If results need to be sorted in reverse order, the client changes the sortOrder value to descending.

Sorting can be combined with filtering and paging to optimize data retrieval. A SCIM request that retrieves the first 50 active users sorted by their usernames would look like /Users?filter=active eq true&sortBy=userName&sortOrder=ascending&startIndex=1&count=50. This request ensures that only active users are returned, sorted alphabetically, and retrieved in manageable batches.

SCIM providers may have limitations on which attributes can be used for sorting. Clients should check the /ServiceProviderConfig endpoint to determine which sorting capabilities are supported. Some providers may allow sorting by multiple attributes, enabling more advanced ordering of results.

Filtering, paging, and sorting work together to optimize SCIM API interactions. Filtering ensures that only relevant records are retrieved, reducing unnecessary data transfers. Paging prevents large responses from overwhelming the API, improving scalability. Sorting organizes results in a meaningful way, enhancing usability and data management. These capabilities enable SCIM clients to process identity data efficiently, making SCIM a scalable solution for modern identity management challenges. Organizations implementing SCIM benefit from improved API performance, reduced resource consumption, and greater flexibility in querying identity records across their applications and services.

SCIM and RESTful API Design

SCIM is built on the principles of RESTful API design, ensuring a lightweight, scalable, and efficient approach to identity management. REST (Representational State Transfer) is an architectural style that defines a set of constraints for building web services, making SCIM highly interoperable across various platforms. By following RESTful principles, SCIM provides a standardized way to create, retrieve, update, and delete identity resources while maintaining compatibility with modern web applications and cloud services.

One of the key characteristics of RESTful API design in SCIM is the use of resource-based endpoints. Each SCIM resource, such as users and groups, is accessed through a well-defined URI structure. The primary endpoints include /Users for managing individual user identities and /Groups for handling collections of users with shared access permissions. These endpoints serve as entry points for SCIM clients to interact with identity data, ensuring that identity management operations are performed consistently.

SCIM relies on standard HTTP methods to perform identity operations. A GET request retrieves identity records, allowing clients to query users, groups, and other resources. A POST request creates a new identity record, while PUT updates an entire resource by replacing its attributes. The PATCH method allows for partial updates, modifying only specific attributes without affecting the entire object. A DELETE request removes a user or group, ensuring that deprovisioned identities no longer have access to connected systems. By leveraging these HTTP methods, SCIM maintains a clear and predictable approach to managing identity data.

A fundamental aspect of RESTful design in SCIM is statelessness, meaning that each request from a client to the SCIM provider must contain all necessary information to process the request. The server does not store client session data between requests, ensuring that SCIM remains scalable and efficient. Stateless interactions simplify API implementation, allowing SCIM providers to handle multiple concurrent requests without requiring complex session management.

SCIM follows a uniform resource structure, ensuring that resource representations remain consistent across different implementations. Each SCIM response is formatted in JSON, a lightweight and widely supported data format. The JSON representation of SCIM resources follows a hierarchical structure, with attributes organized into key-value pairs. Standard attributes such as id, userName, emails, and groups are included in the response, ensuring that SCIM clients can parse identity data easily.

A key advantage of SCIM's RESTful architecture is discoverability, allowing clients to dynamically retrieve service capabilities. The /ServiceProviderConfig endpoint provides metadata about the SCIM implementation, including supported authentication mechanisms, filtering options, sorting capabilities, and version information. This endpoint enables SCIM clients to adjust their API interactions based on the provider's capabilities, improving compatibility and reducing integration complexity.

SCIM supports filtering, sorting, and pagination, essential features of RESTful API design that enhance data retrieval efficiency. The filter parameter allows clients to request only relevant identity records based on attribute values, reducing unnecessary data transfer. The sortBy and sortOrder parameters define how results are ordered, ensuring that SCIM clients receive identity records in a structured manner. Pagination is handled through the startIndex and count parameters, allowing clients to retrieve identity records in smaller batches rather than requesting the entire dataset at once. These features optimize SCIM API performance, ensuring that identity synchronization remains scalable.

RESTful APIs in SCIM follow the principle of self-descriptive messages, meaning that each API request and response contains sufficient metadata to explain its purpose. SCIM responses include HTTP status codes that indicate the success or failure of an operation. A 200 OK status indicates a successful request, while 201 Created confirms the successful creation of a resource. A 400 Bad Request response signals an issue with the client's request, and 401 Unauthorized indicates authentication failure. The use of HTTP status codes improves error handling, allowing SCIM clients to diagnose integration issues effectively.

Another important aspect of RESTful API design in SCIM is hypermedia as the engine of application state (HATEOAS). SCIM responses may include hyperlinks to related resources, enabling clients to navigate identity records efficiently. For example, a user record retrieved from the /Users endpoint may contain a link to their group memberships under /Groups/{id}. These hypermedia controls improve API usability by guiding SCIM clients through available resources dynamically.

SCIM APIs are designed to be extensible, allowing organizations to define custom attributes beyond the standard SCIM schema. The

/Schemas endpoint enables clients to retrieve supported attributes, ensuring that custom extensions are handled correctly. SCIM extensions follow a namespaced structure to avoid conflicts with standard attributes. For example, the enterprise user extension uses the   namespace urn:ietf:params:scim:schemas:extension:enterprise:2.0:User, defining additional attributes such as employeeNumber, costCenter, and manager. This extensibility ensures that SCIM can adapt to industry-specific identity management requirements while maintaining interoperability.

Security is a critical aspect of RESTful API design in SCIM. SCIM enforces authentication and authorization mechanisms to protect identity data. OAuth 2.0 is commonly used for secure authentication, requiring SCIM clients to obtain an access token before making API requests. The token is included in the Authorization header, ensuring that only authorized clients can access SCIM resources. HTTPS is mandatory for all SCIM communications, encrypting data in transit and preventing unauthorized access. Proper access control policies, including role-based access control (RBAC), ensure that SCIM clients can perform only permitted operations.

SCIM adheres to idempotency, an important RESTful design principle that ensures API operations produce consistent results even if the same request is sent multiple times. A PUT request to update a user always results in the same user record state, regardless of how many times the request is issued. This prevents unintended duplicate updates and ensures predictable API behavior. SCIM's PATCH operations allow partial updates while maintaining idempotency, ensuring that changes to individual attributes do not affect other identity data.

Bulk operations in SCIM follow RESTful principles by enabling batch processing of identity modifications through the /Bulk endpoint. A single POST request to this endpoint allows multiple identity operations, including user creation, updates, and deletions, to be executed in sequence. Each operation within the bulk request contains a unique identifier (bulkId), enabling reference between dependent actions. Bulk processing improves efficiency by reducing API call overhead and ensuring that large-scale identity updates are handled in a structured manner.

Error handling in SCIM follows RESTful best practices, ensuring that API clients receive detailed responses when requests fail. SCIM providers return error objects containing status, scimType, and detail fields, providing insights into the cause of the failure. For example, an attempt to create a user with a duplicate userName may return a 409 Conflict response with a detailed error message explaining the issue. Proper error handling improves SCIM integration by helping clients debug issues quickly.

SCIM's RESTful architecture ensures that identity management operations remain consistent, scalable, and efficient. By leveraging resource-based endpoints, HTTP methods, stateless interactions, and standardized responses, SCIM simplifies identity synchronization across different platforms. The use of filtering, sorting, pagination, and bulk operations further enhances SCIM's efficiency, making it well-suited for large-scale identity management. The adoption of RESTful best practices ensures that SCIM remains a flexible and interoperable identity management standard, capable of integrating with a wide range of modern applications and cloud-based services.

SCIM in Cloud Identity Management

SCIM plays a critical role in cloud identity management by providing a standardized and automated way to manage user identities across multiple cloud applications and services. As organizations adopt cloud-based infrastructure and Software-as-a-Service (SaaS) applications, managing user accounts efficiently becomes a challenge. SCIM simplifies identity provisioning, deprovisioning, and synchronization, ensuring that user data remains consistent and secure across different cloud platforms.

Cloud identity management involves the administration of user identities, access controls, and authentication across cloud-based applications. Organizations use cloud identity providers such as Microsoft Entra ID, Google Workspace, and Okta to centralize identity management while enabling seamless access to SaaS applications. Without a standardized protocol like SCIM, integrating multiple identity providers with cloud applications requires custom connectors, complex scripts, and manual intervention. SCIM eliminates these inefficiencies by defining a uniform API for managing user and group data across different systems.

User provisioning in cloud environments is one of the key use cases for SCIM. When an employee joins an organization, their identity must be created in various cloud applications, including email services, collaboration tools, and enterprise resource planning (ERP) systems. SCIM enables automatic provisioning by allowing the identity provider to send a POST request to the /Users endpoint of a cloud service, creating the user account with all necessary attributes. This ensures that employees receive immediate access to required applications, improving productivity and reducing IT overhead.

User deprovisioning is equally important in cloud identity management. When an employee leaves an organization, their access to cloud applications must be revoked to prevent security risks. SCIM automates this process by allowing identity providers to send a DELETE request to the cloud application's SCIM endpoint, ensuring that the user account is removed or deactivated. Some implementations support soft deletion, marking the user as inactive rather than permanently deleting the account. This feature allows for auditability while maintaining compliance with security policies.

SCIM also plays a key role in managing group-based access control in cloud environments. Cloud applications often use groups to assign permissions and enforce role-based access control (RBAC). A SCIM-enabled identity provider can manage groups dynamically by sending POST, PATCH, and DELETE requests to the /Groups endpoint of cloud applications. This allows administrators to automate user group assignments based on job roles, departments, or security policies. When a user is added to a group, SCIM ensures that they automatically inherit the necessary permissions across all connected cloud services.

Cloud applications that integrate SCIM provide real-time identity synchronization, ensuring that user attributes remain up to date. Employees frequently change roles, update contact details, or modify security settings. Without SCIM, these updates would need to be manually propagated across different cloud applications, increasing the risk of inconsistencies. SCIM allows identity providers to send

PATCH requests to modify only the necessary attributes, ensuring that changes are applied instantly without affecting other identity data.

SCIM enhances security in cloud identity management by enforcing centralized authentication and authorization policies. By integrating SCIM with an identity provider, organizations can enforce single sign-on (SSO) and multi-factor authentication (MFA) across multiple cloud services. SCIM ensures that only authenticated and authorized users can access cloud applications, reducing the risk of unauthorized access. Identity policies can be enforced at the identity provider level, ensuring that users comply with security requirements such as password policies and device restrictions before gaining access to cloud applications.

Compliance and regulatory requirements are a major concern in cloud identity management. Organizations must ensure that user data is handled securely and that access to cloud applications is properly controlled. SCIM simplifies compliance by providing a standardized method for auditing and tracking identity changes. The meta.created and meta.lastModified attributes in SCIM user records allow organizations to track when identities were created or updated, ensuring compliance with data retention and security policies. Audit logs can be generated from SCIM API interactions, helping organizations meet regulatory requirements such as GDPR, HIPAA, and SOC 2.

SCIM is particularly beneficial for multi-cloud and hybrid-cloud environments, where organizations use multiple identity providers and cloud applications across different platforms. Managing user identities manually across multiple cloud services is inefficient and prone to errors. SCIM provides a unified identity synchronization mechanism, ensuring that user data remains consistent whether applications are hosted on AWS, Microsoft Azure, Google Cloud, or on-premises infrastructure. By leveraging SCIM, organizations can maintain a centralized identity repository while ensuring seamless integration with cloud applications.

SCIM's ability to support bulk operations further enhances cloud identity management efficiency. When onboarding large numbers of employees or updating access permissions across multiple cloud applications, SCIM's /Bulk endpoint allows identity providers to process multiple create, update, or delete operations in a single request. This reduces API overhead and ensures that identity updates are applied consistently across all integrated cloud services. Bulk operations improve scalability, making SCIM well-suited for enterprises with thousands or millions of users.

Cloud identity providers that implement SCIM provide a self-service user management experience for organizations. Employees can update their own attributes, such as email addresses or phone numbers, and SCIM ensures that these updates propagate across all connected cloud applications automatically. This reduces the workload on IT administrators while maintaining accurate identity records. SCIM also allows for delegated administration, where department managers or team leads can manage user access within their respective groups, improving efficiency and decentralizing identity management.

SCIM supports schema extensions, allowing cloud identity providers and service providers to define custom attributes beyond the standard SCIM schema. Cloud applications in industries such as healthcare, finance, and government may require additional user attributes such as certifications, clearance levels, or compliance-related metadata. SCIM's extensibility ensures that industry-specific identity management needs are met without compromising interoperability with other SCIM-compliant services. The /Schemas endpoint enables identity providers to query supported attributes dynamically, ensuring that custom extensions are properly handled.

Performance optimization is crucial when managing identities in cloud environments. SCIM's support for pagination, filtering, and sorting ensures that identity synchronization remains efficient even in large-scale deployments. The startIndex and count parameters allow identity providers to retrieve user records in batches, preventing performance bottlenecks. The filter parameter enables targeted queries, such as retrieving only active users or users belonging to a specific department. These features reduce API load and improve response times, making SCIM ideal for high-performance cloud identity management.

SCIM improves cloud application onboarding by reducing the complexity of integrating identity management solutions. SaaS vendors that implement SCIM provide customers with a standardized method for syncing users and groups, eliminating the need for custom-built connectors. This improves the adoption of cloud services by simplifying identity integration while reducing operational costs for IT teams. Organizations using SCIM-compliant applications benefit from faster deployments, improved security, and automated identity lifecycle management.

SCIM's role in cloud identity management continues to expand as organizations adopt zero trust security models and identity-first security strategies. SCIM ensures that user access is continuously verified and that identity attributes are dynamically updated based on security policies. By integrating SCIM with cloud identity providers, organizations can implement a least privilege access model, ensuring that users have only the necessary permissions required for their roles. Automated identity revocation prevents over-provisioning, reducing the risk of insider threats and unauthorized access.

SCIM provides a scalable, secure, and standardized approach to cloud identity management by automating identity provisioning, synchronization, and access control across multiple cloud applications. Organizations that implement SCIM benefit from improved security, reduced administrative overhead, and seamless integration between identity providers and cloud services. SCIM's ability to support large-scale identity management operations makes it an essential component of modern cloud security and access governance.

SCIM and Single Sign-On (SSO)

SCIM and Single Sign-On (SSO) are two essential components of modern identity and access management. While SCIM focuses on identity provisioning, deprovisioning, and synchronization, SSO streamlines authentication by allowing users to access multiple applications with a single set of credentials. When implemented together, SCIM and SSO improve security, reduce administrative overhead, and enhance the user experience by ensuring that identities are consistently managed and authentication is seamless across all systems.

SSO eliminates the need for users to remember multiple passwords for different applications. Traditionally, employees and users were required to create separate accounts for each system they accessed, leading to password fatigue and an increased risk of weak or reused passwords. With SSO, users authenticate once through an identity provider (IdP), which then issues secure tokens that grant access to other connected applications. SSO protocols such as Security Assertion Markup Language (SAML) and OpenID Connect (OIDC) are commonly used to establish trust between identity providers and service providers, ensuring that authentication is handled securely.

SCIM complements SSO by automating user provisioning and deprovisioning. While SSO ensures that users can log in with a single identity, SCIM ensures that those identities exist in the target applications. When a new employee joins an organization, SCIM automatically creates their user account in all necessary applications, allowing them to log in via SSO immediately. Without SCIM, administrators would have to manually create accounts in each service, increasing the risk of misconfigurations and inconsistencies. By integrating SCIM with SSO, organizations streamline onboarding and ensure that identity data remains synchronized across all applications.

User lifecycle management is a critical area where SCIM and SSO work together. As employees change roles, their access to applications must be adjusted accordingly. SCIM enables real-time updates to user attributes, ensuring that role-based access control (RBAC) policies remain up to date. If an employee moves to a different department, SCIM updates their group memberships and permissions in all connected applications. When combined with SSO, this ensures that users can only access the applications relevant to their new role without needing manual intervention.

Deprovisioning is another area where SCIM enhances SSO. When an employee leaves an organization, their access must be revoked promptly to prevent unauthorized use of corporate resources. SSO alone does not remove accounts from individual applications; it only prevents further authentication. Without SCIM, deactivated users could retain access to certain applications if their accounts are not manually removed. SCIM automates this process by sending a DELETE request to each connected application, ensuring that user accounts are disabled or deleted when they are no longer needed. This minimizes the risk of orphaned accounts and reduces security vulnerabilities.

SCIM ensures that identity attributes remain consistent across all applications integrated with SSO. Identity providers store key user attributes such as userName, email, givenName, familyName, phoneNumbers, and groups. SCIM synchronizes these attributes with service providers, ensuring that users have the same identity across all applications. This consistency prevents authentication issues that could arise if user attributes were mismatched between the identity provider and the target applications.

Group-based access control is another important function that benefits from SCIM and SSO integration. Many organizations assign application permissions based on group memberships, ensuring that users only have access to relevant resources. SCIM automates group assignments and updates, ensuring that users are added or removed from groups as their roles change. SSO then enforces these permissions, allowing users to authenticate and access applications according to their assigned groups. This integration reduces the risk of over-provisioning, ensuring that users do not retain unnecessary permissions.

SCIM also simplifies SSO implementation for cloud applications and SaaS providers. Many SaaS vendors integrate SSO to improve security and user experience, but managing user accounts in these services can still be a challenge. By adopting SCIM, SaaS providers allow customers to automate user account management, ensuring that users are provisioned and deprovisioned dynamically. This reduces the administrative burden on IT teams and improves the overall efficiency of identity management.

Federated identity management further enhances the combination of SCIM and SSO. In a federated model, organizations rely on a central identity provider to authenticate users across multiple domains. SCIM ensures that user accounts are created and maintained across federated applications, while SSO allows users to authenticate seamlessly across different systems. This approach is especially beneficial in multi-cloud environments, where organizations use multiple identity providers to manage access to cloud services and on-premises applications.

Security improvements are a major advantage of combining SCIM and SSO. Since users authenticate through a single identity provider, organizations can enforce strong authentication policies such as multi-factor authentication (MFA). SCIM ensures that these authentication policies apply consistently across all integrated applications by keeping identity data synchronized. Additionally, organizations can enforce session policies that restrict login access based on location, device, or risk-based authentication rules, further enhancing security.

SCIM also supports Just-In-Time (JIT) provisioning for SSO-enabled applications. JIT provisioning creates user accounts on demand when a user logs in via SSO for the first time. However, JIT provisioning does not handle updates, deprovisioning, or group management efficiently. SCIM complements JIT provisioning by ensuring that user attributes remain updated across all applications and that deactivated users are removed automatically. By integrating SCIM with SSO, organizations achieve a more complete identity management solution.

Auditability and compliance are improved when SCIM and SSO are used together. Organizations must maintain detailed logs of authentication events and identity changes to meet regulatory requirements such as GDPR, HIPAA, and SOC 2. SSO logs authentication attempts, while SCIM logs identity provisioning, updates, and deletions. These logs provide a complete view of user activity, helping organizations detect anomalies, prevent unauthorized access, and demonstrate compliance with security policies.

SCIM's schema extensibility ensures that additional identity attributes can be synchronized alongside SSO authentication. Many organizations require custom attributes such as employeeNumber, costCenter, or manager to be included in user profiles. SCIM allows these attributes to be extended and synchronized across all applications, ensuring that identity records remain comprehensive. This extensibility supports advanced access control policies, ensuring that authentication decisions are based on a complete set of identity attributes.

The integration of SCIM and SSO enhances both user experience and security. Users benefit from seamless access to applications without needing to remember multiple passwords, while administrators gain automated identity management capabilities. Organizations reduce IT workload by eliminating manual account provisioning and improve security by ensuring that deactivated users lose access immediately. SCIM and SSO together create a robust identity management framework, ensuring that user identities remain synchronized while authentication remains secure and seamless.

SCIM and Multi-Factor Authentication (MFA)

SCIM and Multi-Factor Authentication (MFA) play complementary roles in identity management by ensuring secure authentication while maintaining accurate and up-to-date identity records. SCIM focuses on user provisioning, deprovisioning, and synchronization, while MFA enhances authentication security by requiring multiple factors to verify a user's identity. Together, SCIM and MFA create a robust identity and access management framework that improves security, reduces administrative overhead, and ensures compliance with security best practices.

MFA strengthens authentication by requiring users to provide two or more verification factors before accessing an application or system. These factors typically fall into three categories: something the user knows (password or PIN), something the user has (smartphone, security key, or token), and something the user is (biometric data such as fingerprints or facial recognition). By implementing MFA, organizations reduce the risk of unauthorized access, even if user credentials are compromised.

SCIM ensures that identity attributes related to MFA settings remain synchronized across applications and identity providers. Many organizations store MFA-related attributes such as phone numbers for SMS-based authentication, registered authentication devices, and preferred authentication methods. SCIM automates the provisioning and updating of these attributes, ensuring that users have consistent MFA configurations across all connected applications. When a new employee is onboarded, SCIM can automatically enroll them in an MFA system by provisioning their authentication attributes, such as linking their mobile phone number to the identity provider.

Identity providers and authentication services use SCIM to manage user enrollment in MFA policies dynamically. Organizations that enforce adaptive MFA policies may require users to register additional authentication factors based on their role, department, or security requirements. SCIM ensures that these policies are reflected in all integrated systems, preventing inconsistencies where some applications may enforce MFA while others do not. If a user's authentication factor changes, such as switching from SMS-based authentication to a hardware security key, SCIM updates the authentication attributes across all linked services.

Deprovisioning users with MFA-enabled accounts requires careful handling to prevent unauthorized access. When an employee leaves an organization, SCIM ensures that their identity is removed from all connected systems, including MFA authentication providers. Without SCIM, deactivated users might retain access to authentication systems, allowing them to bypass security controls. SCIM automates user deactivation by sending DELETE requests to identity providers, revoking MFA settings, and preventing former employees from authenticating to corporate applications.

SCIM enhances MFA implementations by supporting group-based authentication policies. Many organizations enforce MFA based on user roles or departments, ensuring that privileged accounts require stronger authentication mechanisms than regular users. SCIM automates group assignments, ensuring that users are placed in the correct security policies. For example, SCIM can assign administrators to a high-security MFA policy requiring biometric authentication, while standard employees may only need a one-time password (OTP) via mobile authentication. This integration ensures that security policies remain consistent across different applications.

SCIM's ability to manage authentication attributes extends to integrating with MFA services that use external devices or security keys. Modern authentication methods such as WebAuthn and FIDO2 rely on hardware-based security keys, which must be linked to a user's identity. SCIM synchronizes registered authentication devices across multiple applications, ensuring that users can authenticate consistently across all services. If a user registers a new security key,

SCIM updates the authentication records to reflect the new device, preventing authentication failures due to outdated records.

MFA recovery processes are also improved by SCIM's identity synchronization capabilities. When users lose their authentication devices, they often require alternative authentication methods to regain access. SCIM ensures that backup authentication methods such as backup phone numbers or email addresses remain updated across all systems. If a user changes their backup authentication method, SCIM propagates this change to all MFA-enabled applications, preventing reliance on outdated recovery options.

SCIM helps enforce geolocation-based and risk-based MFA policies by synchronizing user attributes such as location, login history, and device trust levels. Many organizations use adaptive authentication policies where MFA is required only under certain conditions, such as login attempts from unfamiliar locations or untrusted devices. SCIM ensures that risk scores, device registrations, and user session attributes remain consistent across all identity systems, enabling adaptive authentication workflows that reduce friction while maintaining security.

Logging and auditing MFA-related attributes is critical for compliance and security monitoring. Organizations must track changes to authentication settings, including MFA enrollment, device registration, and authentication method updates. SCIM ensures that identity logs capture these changes, providing administrators with a complete record of authentication modifications. Security teams use these logs to detect anomalies such as unauthorized device registrations or sudden changes in authentication behavior. SCIM also integrates with security information and event management (SIEM) solutions, enabling centralized monitoring of authentication and identity management activities.

SCIM supports schema extensions to accommodate additional authentication-related attributes. While the default SCIM schema includes basic identity attributes, organizations can extend it to include MFA-specific fields such as authenticationMethods, trustedDevices, riskLevel, and preferredMFA. These custom attributes ensure that authentication preferences and policies are fully synchronized across all integrated applications. SCIM's extensibility allows organizations to tailor identity management workflows to their specific security requirements while maintaining interoperability with other SCIM-compliant systems.

Cloud-based MFA solutions benefit from SCIM by enabling automated identity synchronization across multiple authentication providers. Organizations using hybrid cloud environments often manage identities across multiple authentication platforms, including Azure Active Directory, Google Workspace, Okta, and Duo Security. SCIM provides a single identity synchronization framework that ensures MFA configurations remain consistent across all platforms. If a user is required to enroll in MFA for one application, SCIM ensures that this requirement is enforced across all linked services, eliminating security gaps caused by inconsistent authentication policies.

SCIM also facilitates self-service MFA enrollment by enabling users to manage their authentication settings across all integrated applications. Many organizations allow employees to update their authentication preferences, such as adding new devices or changing MFA methods. SCIM synchronizes these changes in real time, ensuring that users do not experience authentication failures due to outdated MFA records. This reduces the burden on IT support teams while improving the overall security posture of the organization.

Performance optimization in MFA-enabled environments requires efficient handling of authentication attributes. SCIM's support for pagination, filtering, and sorting ensures that identity synchronization remains efficient even for large user populations. The filter parameter allows identity providers to retrieve only users with specific authentication configurations, such as those enrolled in MFA or requiring reauthentication. The sortBy and sortOrder parameters ensure that identity records are retrieved in a structured manner, reducing processing time for authentication-related queries.

SCIM's integration with MFA ensures that authentication policies remain consistent, security attributes are properly synchronized, and user access is controlled based on the latest identity data. By automating the management of authentication factors, SCIM reduces administrative complexity, improves security, and enhances the user experience across multiple authentication systems. Organizations that combine SCIM with MFA benefit from stronger identity protection, reduced attack surfaces, and seamless user authentication workflows.

SCIM and Role-Based Access Control (RBAC)

SCIM and Role-Based Access Control (RBAC) work together to enforce structured and scalable access management in enterprise environments. SCIM provides a standardized method for provisioning, synchronizing, and deprovisioning user identities, while RBAC ensures that access permissions are assigned based on predefined roles rather than individual users. By integrating SCIM with RBAC, organizations can automate access control, reduce administrative overhead, and enhance security by ensuring that users receive only the permissions necessary for their roles.

RBAC is a security model that assigns access rights based on a user's role within an organization. Instead of granting permissions directly to individuals, access is controlled through roles, which are associated with specific permissions. When a user is assigned to a role, they inherit the permissions linked to that role, ensuring that access is managed consistently. This approach simplifies access management, improves compliance, and reduces the risk of privilege escalation caused by excessive permissions.

SCIM plays a critical role in managing RBAC by synchronizing user-role assignments across multiple applications and services. Identity providers maintain role information as part of user attributes, ensuring that roles are updated dynamically based on organizational changes. When a user is assigned a new role, SCIM propagates this change to all connected systems, ensuring that access rights remain consistent. Without SCIM, administrators would need to manually update user roles in each application, increasing the risk of misconfigurations and security vulnerabilities.

The SCIM schema includes attributes that support RBAC, such as roles, groups, and entitlements. The roles attribute defines a user's assigned roles, while groups represent collections of users who share common permissions. The entitlements attribute stores specific access rights granted to a user, providing granular control over authorization policies. By leveraging these attributes, SCIM ensures that role-based permissions are enforced uniformly across all integrated applications.

User provisioning is a key area where SCIM and RBAC work together. When a new employee joins an organization, SCIM automatically provisions their user account and assigns the appropriate role based on their job function. For example, a new finance employee may be assigned the "Finance Team" role, granting them access to accounting software and financial records. Similarly, an IT administrator may be assigned the "System Administrator" role, allowing them to manage infrastructure and security settings. SCIM ensures that these role assignments are propagated across all connected systems, preventing delays in access provisioning.

Role updates are another critical function supported by SCIM. Employees frequently change roles due to promotions, department transfers, or project assignments. When a user's role changes, SCIM updates their role attribute and synchronizes this change across all applications. This ensures that users receive the correct permissions for their new role while revoking access to resources no longer relevant to their responsibilities. Without SCIM, manual updates would be required, increasing the risk of outdated or excessive permissions remaining in place.

SCIM also facilitates group-based RBAC, where permissions are assigned based on group memberships rather than individual user roles. Many organizations use groups to define access policies, ensuring that all members of a group receive the same level of access. SCIM enables dynamic group management by allowing identity providers to add or remove users from groups automatically. For example, when a new engineer joins the "Development Team" group, SCIM ensures that they inherit access to source code repositories, development tools, and testing environments. If they transition to a different role, SCIM removes them from the group, revoking their previous access privileges.

Deprovisioning users with RBAC is streamlined through SCIM. When an employee leaves an organization, SCIM automatically removes their role and group assignments, ensuring that they no longer have access to corporate resources. A DELETE request sent to the SCIM provider triggers the removal of the user's identity from all connected applications, revoking their permissions immediately. This process minimizes the risk of orphaned accounts, which could be exploited by attackers if not properly deactivated.

SCIM supports hierarchical roles, allowing organizations to define role structures where higher-level roles inherit permissions from lower-level roles. For example, a "Manager" role may include all permissions of the "Employee" role while adding additional administrative capabilities. SCIM ensures that hierarchical role assignments are synchronized consistently, preventing conflicts or unintended privilege escalations. By automating hierarchical role management, organizations reduce the complexity of manual access control configurations.

RBAC policies in SCIM can be extended to include attribute-based access control (ABAC), where access decisions consider user attributes in addition to role assignments. ABAC allows organizations to enforce more dynamic access policies based on contextual factors such as location, department, or project assignment. SCIM synchronizes user attributes such as department, title, and employmentStatus, enabling applications to enforce attribute-based policies. For example, an organization may restrict access to financial records only to users with the "Finance" role and an employmentStatus of "Active." SCIM ensures that these attributes remain updated, preventing unauthorized access based on outdated information.

SCIM enhances auditability and compliance for RBAC implementations by maintaining a consistent record of role assignments and access changes. Organizations must comply with security regulations such as GDPR, HIPAA, and SOC 2, which require strict control over user access. SCIM logs all role-related modifications, including user role assignments, group memberships, and deprovisioning actions. These logs provide valuable insights into access control decisions, helping organizations detect unauthorized privilege changes and ensure compliance with security policies.

Security best practices dictate that least privilege access should be enforced in RBAC implementations, ensuring that users receive only the permissions necessary for their job functions. SCIM helps enforce least privilege access by automating role assignments and revoking excessive permissions when users transition between roles. By preventing over-provisioning of access rights, SCIM reduces the attack surface and minimizes the risk of insider threats.

SCIM supports custom role attributes and schema extensions, allowing organizations to define additional role-related attributes beyond the standard SCIM schema. Some organizations require attributes such as securityClearanceLevel, privilegedAccess, or temporaryAccessExpiration. SCIM enables the synchronization of these attributes, ensuring that custom RBAC policies are enforced consistently across all applications. The /Schemas endpoint allows SCIM clients to query supported attributes dynamically, ensuring that role-specific data is properly handled.

Multi-cloud and hybrid environments benefit from SCIM's ability to synchronize role-based access policies across different platforms. Organizations managing identities across AWS, Microsoft Azure, Google Cloud, and on-premises applications need a consistent way to enforce RBAC. SCIM provides a unified identity synchronization framework that ensures role assignments remain accurate regardless of where applications are hosted. This consistency is essential for preventing access mismatches that could lead to security vulnerabilities.

SCIM also integrates with privileged access management (PAM) solutions, which enforce strict controls over high-privilege accounts. PAM solutions require accurate role definitions to ensure that administrative accounts are properly restricted. SCIM automates privileged role assignments, ensuring that only authorized users receive elevated permissions. If an administrator leaves the organization or transitions to a non-privileged role, SCIM immediately revokes their access to critical systems, reducing the risk of misuse.

SCIM and RBAC together provide a scalable, secure, and automated access management framework. SCIM ensures that user roles and permissions remain synchronized across all applications, reducing administrative workload and improving security. Organizations that implement SCIM with RBAC benefit from streamlined provisioning, dynamic role updates, automated deprovisioning, and enhanced compliance with security regulations. By automating role-based access control through SCIM, organizations create a more efficient and secure identity management system that adapts to changing business needs while minimizing security risks.

SCIM and Attribute-Based Access Control (ABAC)

SCIM and Attribute-Based Access Control (ABAC) work together to create a dynamic, scalable, and secure identity management system. SCIM provides a standardized way to manage user and group attributes, ensuring that identity data remains synchronized across multiple applications. ABAC extends traditional access control models by using attributes such as role, department, location, and security clearance to determine access permissions. By integrating SCIM with ABAC, organizations can automate identity synchronization while enforcing fine-grained access control policies based on user attributes.

ABAC is a security model that grants access based on a combination of user, resource, and environmental attributes. Unlike Role-Based Access Control (RBAC), which assigns permissions based on predefined roles, ABAC evaluates multiple attributes dynamically before granting access. This allows organizations to create more flexible and context-aware access policies. SCIM ensures that these attributes remain consistent and up to date across all applications, preventing unauthorized access caused by outdated or misconfigured identity data.

SCIM plays a critical role in ABAC by synchronizing user attributes that determine access control decisions. The SCIM schema includes standard attributes such as userName, email, givenName, familyName, department, title, organization, and groups. Organizations can also extend the SCIM schema to include custom attributes such as securityClearanceLevel, employmentStatus, projectAssignment, and riskScore. These attributes serve as the foundation for ABAC policies, allowing access control systems to evaluate user characteristics dynamically.

User provisioning is a key area where SCIM and ABAC work together. When a new employee joins an organization, SCIM automatically provisions their account and assigns relevant attributes based on their role, department, and job function. ABAC policies then evaluate these attributes to determine which applications, systems, and resources the user can access. For example, an employee in the finance department may be granted access to financial reporting tools, while an engineer may receive access to source code repositories. By automating attribute assignment through SCIM, organizations reduce the risk of misconfigurations and ensure that access decisions are based on real-time data.

ABAC policies rely on real-time updates to user attributes, making SCIM essential for keeping identity records synchronized. When a user's attributes change, such as a promotion to a managerial role or a transfer to a different department, SCIM propagates these updates across all integrated applications. This ensures that access permissions are adjusted dynamically, preventing security gaps where users retain access to resources they no longer need. Without SCIM, manual updates would be required, increasing the risk of unauthorized access due to outdated attributes.

SCIM also supports group-based ABAC, where user attributes influence group assignments that determine access permissions. Many organizations use groups to enforce access policies, but instead of manually assigning users to groups, SCIM allows dynamic group membership based on attributes. For example, a user with the attribute location eq "New York" may automatically be assigned to the "New York Employees" group, granting them access to location-specific resources. Similarly, users with securityClearanceLevel eq "High" may be assigned to a restricted access group for handling confidential data. This automated approach ensures that users always belong to the correct access groups based on their real-time attributes.

Deprovisioning users in ABAC environments requires accurate attribute management, which SCIM automates. When an employee leaves the organization or their employment status changes to inactive,

SCIM ensures that their attributes are updated across all connected applications. ABAC policies then evaluate this status change and revoke access accordingly. For example, a policy that grants access to internal systems only to users with employmentStatus eq "Active" ensures that deactivated users lose access immediately. This automation prevents lingering access risks and reduces administrative overhead in manually revoking permissions.

ABAC policies can also take into account environmental attributes, such as login location, device type, time of access, and risk level. SCIM can synchronize user device attributes, ensuring that authentication policies account for approved and trusted devices. If a user attempts to access a sensitive application from an unregistered device, an ABAC policy may require additional authentication factors before granting access. SCIM ensures that device attributes remain updated, supporting dynamic and context-aware access control decisions.

SCIM enhances multi-cloud and hybrid identity environments by synchronizing attributes across different platforms. Many organizations manage identities across multiple cloud providers, including AWS, Microsoft Azure, and Google Cloud. SCIM provides a unified identity synchronization framework, ensuring that attributes remain consistent across all environments. This is critical for enforcing ABAC policies across different cloud services, preventing access mismatches that could lead to security vulnerabilities.

Security best practices dictate that least privilege access should be enforced in ABAC implementations. SCIM helps achieve this by ensuring that attributes are updated in real-time, allowing ABAC policies to dynamically adjust permissions based on current user status. For example, an employee working on a temporary project may have an attribute projectAssignment eq "Project X", granting them access to project-specific files. Once the project is completed, SCIM updates the attribute, and ABAC policies automatically revoke access to project resources. This ensures that users retain only the permissions necessary for their job functions, minimizing security risks.

SCIM and ABAC improve auditability and compliance by maintaining a complete record of identity attribute changes. Organizations must comply with security regulations such as GDPR, HIPAA, and SOC 2, which require strict access control policies. SCIM logs all changes to user attributes, including role updates, department changes, and group memberships. ABAC policies then enforce access restrictions based on these attributes. Security teams can analyze SCIM logs to verify that access control decisions align with compliance requirements, detecting unauthorized privilege changes and potential security threats.

SCIM's extensibility allows organizations to define custom attribute mappings that align with their specific ABAC policies. While the standard SCIM schema includes commonly used attributes, organizations may require additional attributes to enforce industry-specific access controls. SCIM supports schema extensions, allowing attributes such as healthcareCertification, financialAccessLevel, or exportControlStatus to be synchronized across all connected applications. These attributes enable organizations to enforce more granular access policies while maintaining interoperability with SCIM-compliant services.

SCIM integrates with policy decision points (PDPs) in ABAC architectures, ensuring that real-time attribute updates influence access control decisions. A PDP evaluates access requests based on ABAC policies, considering user attributes retrieved from SCIM. If a user's attributes change, the PDP enforces updated access rules immediately, preventing access mismatches. SCIM ensures that PDPs receive the latest identity data, reducing latency in enforcing policy changes.

Performance optimization is crucial for large-scale ABAC implementations, where thousands or millions of identity records must be synchronized efficiently. SCIM supports pagination, filtering, and sorting, ensuring that attribute updates are processed efficiently. The filter parameter allows identity providers to retrieve only users who match specific ABAC conditions, such as retrieving all employees with employmentStatus eq "Active". The sortBy and sortOrder parameters ensure that attribute data is retrieved in an optimized manner, reducing API load and improving response times.

SCIM and ABAC together enable organizations to enforce dynamic, attribute-driven access control while maintaining a standardized approach to identity synchronization. SCIM ensures that identity attributes remain updated across all applications, allowing ABAC policies to make accurate access decisions. By integrating SCIM with ABAC, organizations enhance security, improve compliance, and reduce administrative complexity in managing access permissions. SCIM's ability to automate attribute synchronization supports adaptive access control models, ensuring that permissions are granted and revoked in real-time based on current user attributes.

SCIM in Federated Identity Management

SCIM plays a critical role in federated identity management by enabling automated identity provisioning and synchronization across multiple identity domains. Federated identity management allows users to authenticate once and gain access to multiple applications and services, even when they are managed by different organizations or identity providers. SCIM ensures that user identities remain synchronized across these federated environments, preventing inconsistencies and reducing administrative overhead.

Federated identity management is based on the concept of identity federation, where multiple organizations or service providers trust a central identity provider for authentication. Instead of maintaining separate user accounts for each application, users authenticate through a trusted identity provider, which issues authentication tokens to access different services. Protocols such as Security Assertion Markup Language (SAML) and OpenID Connect (OIDC) facilitate authentication in federated environments, while SCIM handles the lifecycle management of user identities.

Authentication in federated identity management does not automatically ensure that user accounts exist in all required applications. SCIM fills this gap by provisioning user accounts dynamically across service providers. When a new user is created in the central identity provider, SCIM automatically provisions their identity in all federated applications, ensuring that they can log in without manual intervention. Without SCIM, administrators would need to create user accounts manually in each service, leading to delays and potential errors.

SCIM also automates user attribute synchronization, ensuring that user profiles remain up to date across all federated applications. Attributes such as email, job title, department, and role must remain consistent across different identity providers and service providers. SCIM ensures that whenever a user's attributes are updated in the central identity provider, these changes are propagated across all federated systems. This prevents inconsistencies where a user's profile differs between applications, which could lead to authentication failures or access issues.

Group management is another critical function that SCIM enhances in federated identity management. Many organizations use groups to manage access to applications and resources, ensuring that users receive the correct permissions based on their roles. SCIM allows identity providers to synchronize group memberships across federated services, ensuring that users automatically receive access to the applications they need. If a user is added to or removed from a group in the central identity provider, SCIM updates their group memberships across all federated applications, maintaining consistent access policies.

SCIM also simplifies the deprovisioning process in federated identity management. When a user leaves an organization or their access needs to be revoked, SCIM ensures that their identity is removed from all federated applications. Without SCIM, user accounts may remain active in some applications, creating security risks due to orphaned accounts. SCIM automates the deprovisioning process by sending a DELETE request to all connected service providers, ensuring that the user's access is revoked instantly.

Federated identity management often involves multiple identity providers, each with its own schema and attribute mappings. SCIM standardizes identity attributes across different providers, ensuring that user data is structured consistently. By using SCIM's predefined schema, organizations can avoid custom integrations that require complex attribute transformations. If an organization needs additional attributes, SCIM allows schema extensions, ensuring that all identity-related information is handled in a standardized way.

Multi-cloud environments benefit significantly from SCIM in federated identity management. Organizations that operate across multiple cloud platforms, such as AWS, Microsoft Azure, and Google Cloud, require a way to synchronize user identities between these environments. SCIM enables seamless identity synchronization, ensuring that users can access resources across different clouds without requiring duplicate account management. This improves security and operational efficiency by maintaining a unified identity framework across all cloud platforms.

SCIM also enhances just-in-time (JIT) provisioning, a common feature in federated identity management. JIT provisioning creates user accounts dynamically when a user logs in for the first time via a federated identity provider. However, JIT provisioning does not handle updates, deprovisioning, or group membership synchronization efficiently. SCIM complements JIT provisioning by ensuring that user accounts remain updated across federated applications, preventing identity drift and reducing the need for manual account management.

Security is a major concern in federated identity management, and SCIM helps enforce security policies across federated applications. Organizations that implement multi-factor authentication (MFA) require consistent identity attributes across all applications. SCIM ensures that authentication-related attributes such as phone numbers, security questions, and authentication device registrations are synchronized across all federated services. This prevents authentication failures caused by missing or outdated security attributes in some applications.

Auditability and compliance are key considerations in federated identity management. Organizations must track identity changes, access provisioning, and deprovisioning activities to meet regulatory requirements. SCIM provides detailed logging of identity synchronization events, ensuring that administrators can monitor user account modifications across all federated applications. These logs help organizations maintain compliance with regulations such as GDPR, HIPAA, and SOC 2 by providing visibility into how user identities are managed.

Federated identity management often involves dynamic access policies based on user attributes, location, and risk levels. SCIM supports attribute-based access control (ABAC), enabling federated identity providers to enforce dynamic access policies based on real-time identity attributes. If a user's risk level changes, SCIM ensures that this update is reflected across all federated applications, enabling security policies to adapt dynamically. This approach strengthens security by ensuring that access decisions are based on the most current identity information.

Performance optimization is critical in large-scale federated identity environments, where thousands or even millions of user accounts must be synchronized across multiple service providers. SCIM supports pagination, filtering, and sorting, ensuring that identity synchronization operations remain efficient. SCIM's filtering capabilities allow federated identity providers to retrieve only the necessary user records based on specific criteria, such as retrieving only active users or users belonging to a particular department. These optimizations improve API performance and reduce synchronization latency.

Organizations that rely on federated identity management often integrate SCIM with identity governance and administration (IGA) solutions to enhance identity lifecycle management. IGA solutions use SCIM to automate user provisioning and enforce governance policies across federated applications. This ensures that identity changes are handled in a structured manner, preventing compliance violations and security risks. SCIM's ability to provide real-time identity synchronization makes it a valuable component of IGA strategies in federated identity environments.

SCIM and federated identity management together create a seamless and secure identity framework that simplifies user account provisioning, synchronization, and deprovisioning across multiple identity domains. By automating identity lifecycle management, SCIM reduces administrative complexity, enhances security, and ensures that users have access to the right applications without delays. Organizations that implement SCIM in federated identity environments benefit from improved efficiency, reduced security risks, and a scalable approach to managing user identities across multiple platforms and service providers.

SCIM and OAuth 2.0

SCIM and OAuth 2.0 work together to provide secure and scalable identity management in modern applications. SCIM focuses on identity provisioning, synchronization, and deprovisioning, while OAuth 2.0 provides a secure authorization framework for granting access to SCIM resources. By integrating SCIM with OAuth 2.0, organizations ensure that only authenticated and authorized clients can perform identity operations, reducing security risks and enforcing access control policies.

OAuth 2.0 is an authorization protocol that allows applications to access resources on behalf of a user or a system without exposing credentials. Instead of sharing passwords, OAuth 2.0 relies on access tokens that represent a client's permission to interact with a protected resource. These tokens are issued by an authorization server and must be included in API requests to authenticate and authorize operations. SCIM adopts OAuth 2.0 as the preferred mechanism for securing API access, ensuring that only authorized clients can create, update, delete, or retrieve identity records.

The OAuth 2.0 flow in SCIM begins with client authentication and token issuance. A SCIM client, such as an identity provider or a service provider, requests an access token from the authorization server by presenting valid credentials. Depending on the security requirements, OAuth 2.0 supports different grant types for obtaining tokens. The client credentials grant is commonly used in SCIM, where a trusted system-to-system interaction requires authentication. In this flow, the SCIM client provides its client ID and client secret to the authorization server, which validates the credentials and returns an access token. This token is then included in the Authorization header of SCIM API requests to prove the client's identity.

Access tokens issued by OAuth 2.0 define the level of access granted to the SCIM client through scopes. Scopes specify what actions a client can perform, such as reading user data, modifying group memberships, or deleting accounts. A SCIM client may request specific scopes during token issuance, and the authorization server determines whether to grant them based on the client's permissions. For example, a client with the scope scim.read can retrieve user records but cannot modify them, while a client with scim.write can create or update users. By enforcing scopes, OAuth 2.0 ensures that SCIM clients operate within their assigned permissions, preventing unauthorized modifications.

Token expiration is an important security measure in OAuth 2.0. Access tokens have a limited lifespan to reduce the risk of misuse if compromised. Once an access token expires, the SCIM client must request a new one using a refresh token, if available. Refresh tokens allow clients to obtain new access tokens without requiring reauthentication, improving security and usability. SCIM implementations must handle token expiration gracefully, rejecting requests with expired tokens and requiring clients to renew authentication. This prevents long-lived tokens from being exploited by attackers.

SCIM and OAuth 2.0 enforce strong authentication mechanisms to protect identity data. OAuth 2.0 supports various authentication methods for securing token requests, including client secrets, mutual TLS, and signed JWT assertions. Public SCIM clients, such as web applications, may use PKCE (Proof Key for Code Exchange) to mitigate token interception risks. Organizations implementing SCIM must choose the appropriate authentication method based on their security policies and compliance requirements. By leveraging OAuth 2.0, SCIM ensures that API access is restricted to trusted clients with valid credentials.

OAuth 2.0 also enhances SCIM's role-based access control (RBAC) by associating tokens with specific roles and policies. When an access token is issued, it may include claims that define the client's role, such as administrator, auditor, or service provider. SCIM providers validate these claims before processing API requests, ensuring that clients only perform actions allowed by their assigned roles. For example, an administrator token may allow user provisioning and deprovisioning, while a read-only token may restrict access to retrieving user information. This role-based enforcement strengthens security by preventing unauthorized privilege escalation.

SCIM clients must handle OAuth 2.0 error responses properly to ensure reliable authentication and authorization workflows. When a SCIM request is denied due to missing or invalid credentials, the SCIM provider returns a 401 Unauthorized response. If the client lacks the necessary permissions for an operation, the provider responds with 403 Forbidden, indicating that the request is not allowed. Error messages should provide clear descriptions to help clients troubleshoot authentication issues, such as invalid tokens, insufficient scopes, or expired credentials. Proper error handling improves the resilience of SCIM integrations, reducing service disruptions caused by authentication failures.

OAuth 2.0 token introspection enables SCIM providers to validate and analyze access tokens before processing API requests. The introspection endpoint allows SCIM providers to query the authorization server for token details, including its validity, expiration time, and associated scopes. This mechanism ensures that SCIM requests use active and authorized tokens, preventing access attempts with revoked or expired credentials. Some implementations also use JWT (JSON Web Token) validation, where the SCIM provider decodes and verifies the token locally without contacting the authorization server, improving performance in high-traffic environments.

Logging and auditing OAuth 2.0 authentication events in SCIM implementations improve security monitoring and compliance. Organizations must track token requests, token usage, and failed authentication attempts to detect potential security threats. OAuth 2.0 logs help identify suspicious activity, such as repeated failed authentication attempts, unauthorized scope requests, or unexpected token usage. SCIM providers should integrate with security information and event management (SIEM) systems to centralize authentication logs and enforce real-time threat detection.

OAuth 2.0 token revocation provides an additional layer of security in SCIM by allowing administrators to invalidate tokens before their expiration time. If a SCIM client is compromised, its tokens can be revoked immediately, preventing further access. SCIM implementations should integrate token revocation mechanisms to ensure that deactivated clients cannot continue performing identity operations. This is especially important in cases of credential leaks or when rotating authentication secrets for security purposes.

OAuth 2.0 also supports delegated authorization, where SCIM clients act on behalf of users with limited permissions. In some scenarios, an administrator may authorize a SCIM client to manage users within a specific department but not modify system-wide settings. Delegated authorization ensures that SCIM clients operate within their assigned privileges, reducing the risk of excessive access. Organizations can implement fine-grained authorization policies by combining OAuth 2.0 with SCIM's attribute-based access control (ABAC), ensuring that token permissions align with identity attributes.

SCIM and OAuth 2.0 together create a secure and efficient identity management framework that ensures authenticated and authorized access to identity resources. SCIM automates user provisioning and synchronization, while OAuth 2.0 enforces access controls through token-based authentication. Organizations benefit from reduced administrative overhead, improved security, and seamless integration with identity providers. By implementing OAuth 2.0 in SCIM, organizations ensure that identity operations remain protected from unauthorized access, aligning with modern security best practices for cloud and enterprise environments.

SCIM and OpenID Connect

SCIM and OpenID Connect (OIDC) work together to provide a seamless and secure identity management solution that automates user provisioning while ensuring strong authentication and authorization. SCIM is designed to handle identity lifecycle management, including provisioning, updating, and deprovisioning users across multiple applications and services. OpenID Connect is an authentication protocol built on OAuth 2.0 that enables users to authenticate securely through an identity provider and access multiple applications without re-entering credentials. By integrating SCIM with OpenID Connect, organizations can achieve both automated identity synchronization and a seamless single sign-on (SSO) experience.

OpenID Connect extends OAuth 2.0 by introducing identity tokens, which contain user authentication information. Unlike OAuth 2.0, which focuses solely on authorization, OpenID Connect provides a standardized method for verifying user identities. When a user logs in using OpenID Connect, the identity provider issues an ID token that contains user claims such as sub (subject identifier), email, name, and preferred_username. These claims allow applications to confirm the user's identity without requiring direct authentication with a username and password. SCIM ensures that these user attributes remain synchronized across all connected systems, reducing identity inconsistencies.

When a user is authenticated through OpenID Connect, their identity attributes may need to be provisioned in multiple applications. SCIM automates this process by creating and updating user records in downstream services. If an organization uses a central identity provider for authentication, OpenID Connect handles the login process, while SCIM provisions the user in applications such as customer relationship management (CRM) systems, enterprise resource planning (ERP) platforms, and collaboration tools. Without SCIM, administrators would need to manually create and manage user accounts in each service, increasing the risk of errors and security vulnerabilities.

SCIM and OpenID Connect improve user onboarding by ensuring that new users gain immediate access to necessary applications. When a user logs in for the first time through OpenID Connect, SCIM provisions their account in all required applications based on their role, department, or group membership. This ensures that employees, contractors, and partners receive the correct level of access without requiring manual intervention. SCIM also updates user attributes dynamically, so changes made at the identity provider level—such as a department transfer or name change—are reflected across all connected applications.

Group-based access control benefits from the integration of SCIM and OpenID Connect. Organizations often define access policies based on group memberships, ensuring that users receive the appropriate permissions. OpenID Connect can include group claims in ID tokens, but it does not handle group membership synchronization. SCIM complements OpenID Connect by ensuring that group memberships are consistently maintained across all applications. If a user is added to or removed from a group in the identity provider, SCIM propagates the change to downstream applications, ensuring that access permissions remain aligned with organizational policies.

Just-in-time (JIT) provisioning is a feature of OpenID Connect that creates user accounts dynamically when a user logs in for the first time. While JIT provisioning is useful for reducing administrative overhead, it has limitations in managing user updates and deprovisioning. JIT provisioning only creates a user account at the time of authentication but does not synchronize attribute changes or remove users when they leave an organization. SCIM addresses these limitations by ensuring that user records are continuously updated and deprovisioned as needed, maintaining consistency across all connected systems.

SCIM ensures that user deprovisioning is handled correctly when OpenID Connect is used for authentication. When an employee leaves an organization or no longer requires access to specific applications, SCIM removes or disables their account across all integrated services. OpenID Connect alone does not manage user lifecycle events such as account termination, which can lead to security risks if inactive accounts remain accessible. SCIM automates deprovisioning by sending DELETE or PATCH requests to connected applications, ensuring that user access is revoked in a timely manner.

Security is enhanced when SCIM and OpenID Connect are integrated. OpenID Connect enables secure authentication using multi-factor authentication (MFA) and adaptive authentication policies, ensuring that users authenticate through a trusted identity provider. SCIM ensures that identity attributes used for authentication, such as phone numbers, device registrations, and risk scores, are synchronized across all applications. This prevents authentication failures caused by outdated or inconsistent identity data.

Access token validation is a key component of OpenID Connect that helps secure API interactions. When a user authenticates through OpenID Connect, they receive an access token that authorizes them to access specific resources. SCIM can use OpenID Connect's token introspection endpoint to verify whether an access token is valid before performing identity operations. If a token is expired or revoked, SCIM denies the request, preventing unauthorized modifications to identity records.

Auditability and compliance are strengthened when SCIM and OpenID Connect are used together. Organizations must track user authentication events and identity changes to meet regulatory requirements such as GDPR, HIPAA, and SOC 2. OpenID Connect logs authentication attempts, while SCIM logs identity provisioning, updates, and deprovisioning activities. These logs provide a complete view of user lifecycle events, allowing organizations to detect unauthorized access, investigate security incidents, and demonstrate compliance with industry regulations.

Multi-cloud and hybrid environments benefit from the integration of SCIM and OpenID Connect. Many organizations manage identities across multiple identity providers and cloud platforms, requiring a standardized approach to authentication and identity synchronization. OpenID Connect provides a common authentication layer across different cloud providers, while SCIM ensures that user attributes remain consistent across all platforms. This eliminates identity silos and prevents access discrepancies between different cloud services.

SCIM supports schema extensions that allow organizations to synchronize additional user attributes beyond the default OpenID Connect claims. Some applications require attributes such as employee numbers, security clearance levels, or contract expiration dates to enforce access control policies. SCIM ensures that these attributes are synchronized across all applications, allowing organizations to implement granular access policies based on real-time identity data. By defining custom schemas, organizations can extend SCIM's functionality while maintaining interoperability with OpenID Connect.

SCIM and OpenID Connect together provide a powerful identity management framework that automates user provisioning, enhances authentication security, and ensures consistency across multiple applications. OpenID Connect handles user authentication, ensuring that users log in through a centralized identity provider, while SCIM synchronizes identity data across all connected services. Organizations that integrate SCIM with OpenID Connect benefit from reduced administrative overhead, improved security, and a seamless user experience. By leveraging both protocols, businesses achieve a unified identity management strategy that supports scalable and secure access control across cloud and enterprise environments.

SCIM and LDAP Integration

SCIM and LDAP integration enables organizations to bridge modern identity management standards with legacy directory services. SCIM provides a REST-based approach to user provisioning and synchronization, while LDAP (Lightweight Directory Access Protocol) is a widely used protocol for managing user identities in on-premises directory services such as Microsoft Active Directory (AD) and OpenLDAP. Integrating SCIM with LDAP allows organizations to automate identity lifecycle management while maintaining compatibility with existing directory-based authentication and authorization systems.

LDAP has been the foundation of enterprise identity management for decades, offering a structured and hierarchical way to store user and group information. Many organizations rely on LDAP directories to authenticate users, enforce access controls, and manage organizational hierarchies. However, LDAP lacks a standardized API for provisioning users across cloud services and modern applications. SCIM fills this gap by providing a uniform protocol that enables LDAP directories to interact seamlessly with cloud-based identity providers, SaaS applications, and federated identity systems.

SCIM acts as a provisioning layer that synchronizes user data between LDAP directories and external applications. When a new user is added to an LDAP directory, SCIM ensures that the user's identity is provisioned in all necessary cloud services. This eliminates the need for manual account creation in multiple applications, reducing administrative overhead and minimizing the risk of errors. SCIM retrieves user attributes from LDAP and translates them into SCIM-compliant attributes before sending them to connected applications.

User attribute mapping is a key aspect of SCIM and LDAP integration. LDAP directories store user data in structured attributes such as cn (common name), sn (surname), mail, uid, and memberOf (group membership). SCIM uses a standardized schema with attributes such as userName, givenName, familyName, emails, and groups. To enable seamless synchronization, SCIM implementations must define mappings between LDAP attributes and SCIM attributes. For example, the LDAP attribute mail maps to SCIM's emails.value, while uid maps to userName. Proper attribute mapping ensures that identity data remains consistent across systems.

SCIM simplifies user updates and modifications by automatically propagating LDAP changes to connected applications. When a user's department, job title, or contact information is updated in LDAP, SCIM synchronizes these changes in real time, ensuring that all integrated services reflect the latest identity data. Without SCIM, administrators would need to manually update each application, leading to potential inconsistencies and outdated user profiles.

Group management is another area where SCIM enhances LDAP functionality. Many organizations use LDAP groups to assign access permissions to applications and resources. SCIM extends this capability by synchronizing LDAP group memberships with external applications, ensuring that users have the correct access privileges. When a user is added to or removed from an LDAP group, SCIM updates the user's group memberships in all connected services, enforcing role-based access control (RBAC) policies consistently across cloud and on-premises environments.

SCIM also streamlines user deprovisioning in LDAP environments. When an employee leaves an organization, their account must be disabled or removed from LDAP, and access to all associated applications must be revoked. SCIM automates this process by detecting user deletions or status changes in LDAP and propagating them to external applications. This prevents orphaned accounts and reduces security risks associated with inactive users retaining access to critical systems.

SCIM supports bidirectional synchronization with LDAP, allowing organizations to maintain a single source of truth for identity data. In some cases, LDAP serves as the authoritative identity store, and SCIM synchronizes changes to cloud applications. In other cases, a cloud identity provider such as Microsoft Entra ID (formerly Azure AD) acts as the primary identity source, with SCIM updating LDAP directories to reflect changes. This flexibility allows organizations to integrate legacy LDAP systems with modern identity platforms while ensuring data consistency.

Authentication and authorization in LDAP environments can be enhanced with SCIM by synchronizing identity attributes required for authentication policies. Many organizations enforce authentication rules based on attributes such as memberOf, employeeType, or securityLevel. SCIM ensures that these attributes remain updated across all applications, allowing authentication systems to apply policies consistently. If a user is promoted to a new role, SCIM updates the necessary attributes in LDAP and synchronizes them with federated authentication services, preventing unauthorized access.

Security and compliance requirements drive the need for auditability and logging in identity management. Organizations must track user provisioning, role assignments, and deprovisioning activities to comply with regulations such as GDPR, HIPAA, and SOC 2. SCIM provides logging and audit capabilities that track changes to identity records, ensuring that administrators can monitor and review identity updates. LDAP directories also maintain logs of authentication and access events, and integrating SCIM with these logs provides a comprehensive view of identity changes across the organization.

Multi-cloud and hybrid identity architectures benefit from SCIM and LDAP integration by enabling centralized identity management across different platforms. Many enterprises operate hybrid environments where LDAP directories manage on-premises identities while cloud identity providers handle SaaS and cloud-native applications. SCIM ensures seamless synchronization between these environments, allowing users to authenticate and access applications regardless of where their identity is stored.

SCIM's support for filtering and pagination improves the efficiency of LDAP synchronization. Instead of retrieving all LDAP users and groups at once, SCIM allows incremental updates using filter parameters to select specific records. For example, SCIM can request only active users by filtering on the employeeStatus attribute or retrieve only users who have changed since the last synchronization. Pagination reduces the load on LDAP servers by fetching identity records in manageable batches, improving performance and scalability.

Organizations implementing SCIM with LDAP must consider schema extensions to accommodate custom attributes required for business operations. LDAP directories often include organization-specific attributes such as divisionCode, contractStatus, or accessLevel. SCIM supports schema extensions, allowing these attributes to be mapped and synchronized with external applications. The /Schemas endpoint in SCIM enables dynamic discovery of supported attributes, ensuring interoperability between LDAP and SCIM-compliant services.

SCIM integration with LDAP also enhances just-in-time (JIT) provisioning for applications that rely on LDAP authentication. When a user authenticates against an LDAP directory for the first time, SCIM can provision their account in downstream applications, reducing manual onboarding tasks. JIT provisioning is particularly useful in environments where access is granted dynamically based on LDAP attributes, ensuring that users can access required services without administrative intervention.

SCIM and LDAP together create a comprehensive identity management solution that combines the strengths of directory-based authentication with modern identity provisioning standards. Organizations leveraging SCIM and LDAP integration benefit from automated identity synchronization, improved access control, reduced administrative overhead, and enhanced security. By bridging legacy directory services with cloud-based identity management, SCIM enables enterprises to maintain a unified identity framework across both traditional and modern IT environments.

SCIM in Hybrid Cloud Environments

SCIM plays a crucial role in hybrid cloud environments by enabling seamless identity synchronization across on-premises and cloud-based applications. Organizations increasingly adopt hybrid cloud strategies to balance the control of on-premises infrastructure with the scalability and flexibility of cloud services. Managing user identities across multiple environments can be challenging without a standardized approach. SCIM simplifies identity provisioning, updates, and deprovisioning by ensuring that user data remains consistent across all systems, regardless of whether they are hosted on-premises or in the cloud.

Hybrid cloud environments combine private cloud, public cloud, and on-premises systems to create a flexible and scalable IT architecture. Many organizations continue to rely on traditional identity directories such as Microsoft Active Directory (AD) or LDAP for user authentication and access management while integrating cloud-based identity providers such as Microsoft Entra ID (formerly Azure AD), Okta, or Google Workspace for modern applications. SCIM bridges these systems by providing a common identity synchronization protocol, ensuring that user attributes, roles, and permissions remain consistent across different platforms.

User provisioning in hybrid cloud environments is one of the key challenges that SCIM addresses. When a new employee joins an organization, their identity must be created across multiple systems, including on-premises directories, cloud applications, and SaaS platforms. SCIM automates this process by provisioning user accounts in all necessary environments based on predefined policies. Instead of manually creating accounts in each system, SCIM enables organizations to define provisioning workflows that automatically create, update, and deactivate users across all connected services.

User attribute synchronization ensures that identity records remain up to date in a hybrid cloud environment. Organizations must maintain accurate user details, such as email addresses, phone numbers, job titles, and department information, across all applications. SCIM synchronizes these attributes dynamically, preventing inconsistencies that can lead to authentication issues and access control failures. If an employee's job title or department changes, SCIM ensures that this update propagates across both on-premises and cloud-based systems, reducing the risk of outdated user records.

SCIM also facilitates group-based access control in hybrid cloud environments. Many organizations define access policies based on group memberships, ensuring that users have the correct permissions for applications and resources. SCIM synchronizes group memberships between on-premises directories and cloud services, ensuring that users are automatically assigned or removed from groups based on their role or department. If an organization manages user groups in Active Directory but relies on cloud-based applications for collaboration, SCIM ensures that group assignments remain consistent across both environments.

Deprovisioning users in a hybrid cloud environment can be complex without SCIM. When an employee leaves an organization, their access to all on-premises and cloud-based applications must be revoked to prevent security risks. SCIM automates this process by detecting user terminations in an authoritative identity source, such as an HR system or Active Directory, and propagating account deactivation or deletion across all connected applications. This prevents orphaned accounts and reduces the risk of unauthorized access caused by inactive users retaining system privileges.

SCIM's bidirectional synchronization capabilities allow organizations to integrate multiple identity sources within a hybrid cloud environment. In some cases, an on-premises Active Directory serves as the primary identity source, with SCIM synchronizing users to cloud applications. In other cases, a cloud identity provider such as Okta or Microsoft Entra ID may act as the authoritative identity source, with SCIM ensuring that on-premises directories reflect changes made in the cloud. This flexibility enables organizations to implement identity management policies that align with their security and compliance requirements.

Security and compliance are key considerations in hybrid cloud environments, and SCIM plays a vital role in enforcing identity governance policies. Organizations must ensure that user access is granted and revoked according to security policies, regulatory requirements, and business rules. SCIM supports compliance by maintaining detailed audit logs of identity changes, including account provisioning, modifications, and deletions. These logs provide visibility into identity management activities, enabling organizations to detect unauthorized changes, investigate security incidents, and meet regulatory reporting requirements.

Multi-factor authentication (MFA) is commonly used to enhance security in hybrid cloud environments, requiring users to verify their identity using additional authentication factors such as mobile devices, security keys, or biometrics. SCIM ensures that MFA-related attributes, such as phone numbers for SMS-based authentication or registered authentication devices, are synchronized across all systems. This prevents authentication failures caused by mismatched identity attributes between on-premises and cloud-based authentication services.

SCIM optimizes performance in hybrid cloud environments by supporting filtering, pagination, and incremental updates. Instead of synchronizing all users and attributes every time an update occurs, SCIM allows organizations to retrieve only the necessary changes using filtering and pagination parameters. This improves API efficiency, reduces network bandwidth usage, and ensures that identity synchronization processes do not overload system resources. By implementing incremental synchronization, organizations can maintain real-time identity updates without unnecessary data transfers.

Hybrid cloud environments often involve integrating legacy applications that do not natively support modern identity protocols such as OpenID Connect or OAuth 2.0. SCIM extends identity management to these applications by acting as a provisioning bridge. Organizations can implement SCIM-based provisioning connectors that interact with legacy applications, ensuring that user accounts are created, updated, and removed consistently across all systems. This enables organizations to modernize their identity management processes without requiring extensive application rewrites.

SCIM enables identity lifecycle automation by integrating with identity governance and administration (IGA) platforms. IGA solutions help organizations enforce role-based access controls, manage user certifications, and monitor compliance with access policies. SCIM enhances IGA capabilities by synchronizing identity changes in real time, ensuring that users receive the correct permissions based on their job function and business requirements. This integration improves efficiency by reducing the manual effort required to manage user access across hybrid cloud environments.

SCIM also supports schema extensions, allowing organizations to define custom identity attributes that are specific to their business needs. While SCIM defines a standard schema for user attributes, many organizations require additional attributes such as project assignments, contractor status, or security clearance levels. SCIM schema extensions enable these attributes to be synchronized across all systems, ensuring that custom identity information is available where needed. This flexibility allows organizations to implement identity policies tailored to their industry and regulatory requirements.

Hybrid cloud adoption continues to grow as organizations seek to balance security, scalability, and flexibility. SCIM provides a standardized identity synchronization framework that simplifies user provisioning, updates, and deprovisioning across both on-premises and cloud environments. By integrating SCIM with hybrid identity architectures, organizations reduce administrative complexity, improve security, and ensure that user identities remain consistent across all applications and services. SCIM's ability to automate identity management processes enhances operational efficiency and supports compliance with evolving security and regulatory requirements.

SCIM for SaaS Applications

SCIM provides a standardized approach for managing user identities in SaaS applications by automating user provisioning, updates, and deprovisioning. SaaS applications rely on identity data to control access, enforce security policies, and ensure compliance with organizational requirements. Without SCIM, managing user accounts across multiple SaaS platforms requires manual intervention, custom scripts, or proprietary APIs, leading to inefficiencies and potential security risks. SCIM simplifies identity management by providing a consistent, REST-based API that enables seamless integration between identity providers and SaaS applications.

SaaS applications often serve diverse user populations, including employees, contractors, and external partners. Organizations must ensure that users have access to the right applications based on their role and business needs. SCIM automates the provisioning process by creating user accounts in SaaS applications as soon as they are added to the organization's identity provider. When a new employee joins a company, SCIM ensures that their identity is provisioned across all necessary SaaS applications, reducing delays and eliminating manual account creation tasks.

SCIM ensures that user attributes remain synchronized between the identity provider and SaaS applications. User information such as name, email, job title, department, and phone number must remain consistent across multiple platforms. If an employee's job title changes or they move to a different department, SCIM propagates these updates automatically to all connected SaaS applications. This prevents inconsistencies where outdated user attributes could cause authentication failures or incorrect access permissions.

SaaS applications often use group-based access control to assign permissions based on user roles. SCIM synchronizes group memberships, ensuring that users receive the appropriate level of access based on their organizational role. If an organization manages group assignments in its identity provider, SCIM ensures that those group memberships are reflected in SaaS applications. When a user is added to a group in the identity provider, SCIM updates the user's role in the SaaS platform, granting the necessary permissions. Similarly, if a user is removed from a group, SCIM ensures that their access is adjusted accordingly.

User deprovisioning is a critical function in SaaS identity management. When an employee leaves an organization or no longer requires access to a specific application, their account must be deactivated or removed from all SaaS platforms. SCIM automates this process by detecting when a user is deactivated in the identity provider and propagating that change to all connected SaaS applications. This prevents unauthorized access by ensuring that former employees or contractors do not retain active accounts in business-critical applications.

SCIM improves security in SaaS applications by enforcing identity governance policies. Organizations must ensure that only authorized users have access to SaaS platforms and that permissions are updated in real time. SCIM supports compliance by maintaining audit logs of user provisioning, modifications, and deprovisioning activities. Security teams can use these logs to track identity changes, detect unauthorized access attempts, and enforce regulatory requirements such as GDPR, HIPAA, and SOC 2.

SaaS vendors that implement SCIM provide customers with a seamless identity integration experience. Many enterprises require identity federation between their internal directories and external SaaS applications. By supporting SCIM, SaaS vendors enable organizations to connect their existing identity providers without the need for custom API integrations. This reduces implementation time, lowers integration costs, and improves the overall adoption of SaaS applications in enterprise environments.

SCIM also facilitates just-in-time (JIT) provisioning, allowing SaaS applications to create user accounts dynamically when users log in for the first time. While JIT provisioning eliminates the need for pre-provisioning user accounts, it has limitations in managing attribute updates and deprovisioning users. SCIM enhances JIT provisioning by ensuring that user attributes are continuously synchronized and that accounts are deactivated when users leave the organization. This prevents identity drift, where user information becomes outdated over time due to manual management.

SaaS applications that integrate SCIM benefit from improved performance and scalability. SCIM supports pagination, filtering, and incremental updates, allowing SaaS platforms to retrieve only the necessary user data without overloading system resources. Instead of syncing all users in an organization at once, SCIM enables SaaS applications to process updates in smaller batches, improving API efficiency and reducing synchronization latency. Filtering capabilities allow SaaS applications to request specific subsets of users based on attributes such as department, role, or employment status.

SCIM also supports schema extensions, allowing SaaS vendors to define custom attributes that align with their application-specific requirements. While SCIM provides a standard schema for user attributes, some SaaS platforms require additional fields such as customer-specific roles, subscription tiers, or custom metadata. SCIM schema extensions enable SaaS applications to synchronize these attributes seamlessly without deviating from the core SCIM standard. The /Schemas endpoint allows identity providers to discover supported attributes dynamically, ensuring compatibility across different implementations.

Multi-factor authentication (MFA) is commonly enforced in SaaS applications to enhance security. SCIM ensures that MFA-related attributes, such as registered authentication devices or secondary email addresses, are synchronized between the identity provider and SaaS platforms. This prevents authentication failures caused by mismatched security settings and ensures that users can authenticate seamlessly across multiple applications. SaaS applications that enforce risk-based authentication policies benefit from SCIM's ability to update user attributes dynamically, allowing access decisions to be based on real-time identity data.

SaaS applications operating in hybrid and multi-cloud environments require consistent identity synchronization across multiple platforms. SCIM enables SaaS vendors to integrate with both cloud-based and on-premises identity providers, ensuring that user data remains consistent regardless of where authentication occurs. Organizations using a mix of Microsoft Entra ID, Okta, Google Workspace, and on-premises LDAP directories can use SCIM to unify identity management across all SaaS applications.

SaaS vendors that implement SCIM gain a competitive advantage by offering customers an industry-standard identity management solution. Many enterprise customers require SCIM support as part of their SaaS adoption strategy to reduce administrative complexity and improve security. By providing SCIM-based provisioning, SaaS vendors eliminate the need for customers to build and maintain custom identity connectors, accelerating deployment and reducing operational costs. SaaS applications that natively support SCIM are more attractive to large enterprises with complex identity management needs.

SCIM enhances identity lifecycle management in SaaS applications by providing a standardized, automated, and secure approach to user provisioning. SaaS platforms that integrate SCIM benefit from streamlined onboarding, improved security, and reduced administrative overhead. Organizations leveraging SCIM for SaaS identity management gain greater control over user access, ensuring that accounts are created, updated, and deactivated in a consistent and efficient manner. SaaS vendors that adopt SCIM improve their interoperability with enterprise identity providers, enabling seamless integration and enhancing the overall customer experience.

SCIM and Active Directory Integration

SCIM provides a modern, standardized approach to identity management, while Active Directory (AD) remains the backbone of many enterprise authentication and authorization systems. Integrating SCIM with Active Directory enables organizations to automate user provisioning, attribute synchronization, and deprovisioning across on-premises and cloud-based applications. SCIM acts as a bridge between Active Directory and cloud identity providers, ensuring that user data remains consistent across all environments while reducing manual administrative tasks.

Active Directory is a directory service developed by Microsoft that stores user identities, groups, policies, and authentication details. Many organizations rely on AD to manage employee access to internal applications and resources. However, as businesses adopt cloud applications and SaaS platforms, they face challenges in synchronizing AD users with external identity systems. SCIM addresses this challenge by providing a REST-based API that enables seamless identity synchronization between Active Directory and cloud applications.

User provisioning in Active Directory environments often requires administrators to manually create accounts in multiple systems, leading to delays and inconsistencies. SCIM automates this process by detecting new users in AD and provisioning them in connected applications. When an employee is added to Active Directory, SCIM synchronizes their identity with cloud services such as Microsoft Entra ID (formerly Azure AD), Okta, Google Workspace, and various SaaS applications. This ensures that new employees gain immediate access to the applications they need without manual intervention.

SCIM ensures that user attributes remain consistent between Active Directory and cloud-based applications. Active Directory stores user attributes such as sAMAccountName, mail, givenName, sn, and memberOf, which must be mapped to SCIM attributes like userName, emails.value, givenName, familyName, and groups. Attribute mapping ensures that identity data is correctly synchronized across all systems. If an employee updates their phone number, email address, or job title in Active Directory, SCIM propagates these changes to cloud applications, preventing outdated user information from causing authentication or access issues.

Group management is critical for enforcing access control in Active Directory environments. Many organizations use AD groups to manage user permissions for internal applications and file shares. SCIM extends group management to cloud applications by synchronizing AD group memberships with external identity providers and SaaS platforms. When a user is added to or removed from an AD group, SCIM updates their access in connected applications, ensuring that permissions remain aligned across all systems. This automation reduces the administrative burden of managing group memberships manually and prevents discrepancies in access rights.

User deprovisioning is an essential security measure in identity management. When an employee leaves an organization, their AD account is typically disabled or deleted. SCIM automates this process by propagating user deactivation to all connected applications, ensuring that access is revoked immediately. Without SCIM, organizations must manually remove user accounts from multiple systems, increasing the risk of orphaned accounts that could be exploited by attackers. By integrating SCIM with Active Directory, organizations enhance security by enforcing real-time deprovisioning across all identity systems.

SCIM supports bidirectional synchronization between Active Directory and cloud identity providers. In some cases, Active Directory serves as the authoritative identity source, with SCIM syncing users and groups to cloud applications. In other cases, a cloud identity provider such as Microsoft Entra ID or Okta acts as the primary identity store, with SCIM ensuring that AD reflects changes made in the cloud. This flexibility allows organizations to implement hybrid identity management strategies that align with their security and operational requirements.

Multi-factor authentication (MFA) is commonly enforced in Active Directory environments to enhance security. SCIM ensures that MFA-related attributes, such as phone numbers for SMS-based authentication or registered authentication devices, remain synchronized between AD and cloud applications. This prevents authentication failures caused by mismatched security settings and ensures a seamless authentication experience for users accessing both on-premises and cloud-based resources.

SCIM also enables just-in-time (JIT) provisioning for applications that authenticate users against Active Directory. When a user logs into a cloud application using their AD credentials, SCIM can provision their account dynamically in the target system, reducing the need for pre-created accounts. JIT provisioning eliminates onboarding delays while ensuring that users receive access only when needed. SCIM enhances JIT provisioning by managing attribute updates and deprovisioning users when their AD status changes.

Security and compliance are major concerns in organizations that use Active Directory as their primary identity system. SCIM helps enforce security policies by ensuring that identity attributes are consistently updated and access controls are properly maintained. Organizations must comply with regulations such as GDPR, HIPAA, and SOC 2, which require strict identity governance. SCIM supports compliance by maintaining audit logs of user provisioning, updates, and deletions, allowing administrators to monitor identity changes and detect unauthorized access attempts.

SCIM optimizes performance in Active Directory integrations by supporting filtering, pagination, and incremental updates. Instead of synchronizing all AD users and groups in bulk, SCIM retrieves only the necessary records based on predefined filters. Organizations can configure SCIM to sync only active users, employees from specific departments, or users with recent attribute changes. Pagination ensures that large identity directories are synchronized efficiently without overloading system resources, improving API performance and scalability.

SCIM enables organizations to extend Active Directory's identity management capabilities beyond on-premises applications. Many legacy applications rely on AD for authentication but do not support modern identity protocols such as OAuth 2.0 or OpenID Connect. SCIM acts as a provisioning layer, allowing organizations to integrate legacy applications with cloud-based identity providers. By implementing SCIM-based connectors, organizations can extend

Active Directory identities to SaaS applications, ensuring consistent user management across all environments.

Hybrid cloud architectures benefit from SCIM's ability to synchronize Active Directory identities with multiple cloud platforms. Organizations using a combination of Microsoft Azure, AWS, and Google Cloud require a standardized approach to identity management. SCIM provides a unified identity synchronization framework that ensures AD users can access cloud-based applications without requiring duplicate account management. By centralizing identity provisioning through SCIM, organizations reduce complexity and maintain a consistent security posture across hybrid environments.

SCIM schema extensions allow organizations to define custom identity attributes that are not included in the default schema. While SCIM provides standard attributes for user profiles, many organizations require additional attributes such as employeeNumber, securityClearanceLevel, or projectAssignment. SCIM supports schema extensions, enabling organizations to synchronize custom attributes across Active Directory and cloud applications. The /Schemas endpoint in SCIM allows identity providers to query supported attributes dynamically, ensuring interoperability across different systems.

Organizations that integrate SCIM with Active Directory achieve greater automation, security, and efficiency in identity management. SCIM eliminates manual account provisioning, ensures real-time attribute synchronization, enforces group-based access controls, and automates user deprovisioning. By providing a standardized identity synchronization framework, SCIM enables organizations to bridge the gap between traditional Active Directory environments and modern cloud-based applications, ensuring seamless identity management across all platforms.

SCIM in DevOps and CI/CD

SCIM plays an essential role in modern DevOps and Continuous Integration/Continuous Deployment (CI/CD) environments by automating identity and access management across development pipelines, cloud platforms, and containerized infrastructures. As DevOps practices emphasize automation, speed, and scalability, managing user identities and permissions manually becomes inefficient and error-prone. SCIM provides a standardized way to synchronize user accounts, roles, and permissions across various tools and services, ensuring that development teams maintain secure access without delays or inconsistencies.

CI/CD pipelines rely on automated workflows to build, test, and deploy applications efficiently. These workflows often involve multiple services, including code repositories, build servers, cloud environments, and monitoring tools. Each service requires identity management to ensure that only authorized users and automated processes have access. SCIM simplifies identity provisioning and deprovisioning in CI/CD environments by ensuring that developer and service accounts are created and updated dynamically. When a new developer joins a team, SCIM provisions their access to version control systems such as GitHub, GitLab, or Bitbucket, as well as CI/CD tools like Jenkins, CircleCI, and GitHub Actions.

SCIM improves security in DevOps by enforcing role-based access control (RBAC) and attribute-based access control (ABAC) across development tools. Many organizations define access policies based on job roles, ensuring that developers, testers, and release engineers have the correct permissions for their tasks. SCIM synchronizes these roles with DevOps tools, preventing unauthorized privilege escalation. If a developer is promoted to a lead engineer, SCIM ensures that their new role is reflected across all integrated platforms, granting them additional permissions without requiring manual intervention.

Infrastructure as Code (IaC) is a core principle of DevOps that enables teams to define and manage infrastructure using code. Identity management must also align with this automation strategy. SCIM allows organizations to manage developer identities, access policies, and machine accounts as code, ensuring that changes to identity configurations are version-controlled and auditable. DevOps teams can use SCIM-compatible APIs to automate the creation and removal of service accounts in cloud environments, reducing the risk of orphaned accounts and unauthorized access.

Cloud-based CI/CD pipelines benefit from SCIM's ability to synchronize identities across multiple environments. Many development teams use hybrid or multi-cloud architectures, deploying applications across AWS, Azure, Google Cloud, and Kubernetes clusters. SCIM ensures that user access remains consistent across these platforms, reducing the complexity of managing credentials and permissions in different cloud environments. If a developer requires temporary access to a production environment for debugging, SCIM can grant and revoke access dynamically based on pre-defined policies.

SCIM also enhances security in DevOps by automating the deprovisioning of users and service accounts. When a developer leaves the organization or transitions to a different team, SCIM removes their access from all connected DevOps tools, preventing lingering permissions that could lead to security vulnerabilities. Organizations that use temporary accounts for contractors and consultants can configure SCIM to enforce expiration policies, ensuring that access is automatically revoked after a set period.

CI/CD environments frequently rely on secrets management solutions to store API keys, encryption keys, and other sensitive credentials. SCIM ensures that only authorized identities can access these secrets by synchronizing identity attributes with security tools such as HashiCorp Vault, AWS Secrets Manager, and Azure Key Vault. When a user's access level changes, SCIM updates their permissions in these secrets management systems, preventing unauthorized retrieval of sensitive data.

Containerized applications deployed in Kubernetes clusters require strict identity and access management to prevent unauthorized access to workloads. SCIM helps manage Kubernetes identities by synchronizing user roles and permissions with Kubernetes Role-Based Access Control (RBAC) policies. When a new developer joins a team, SCIM ensures that they are automatically assigned the correct Kubernetes roles, enabling them to deploy and manage containers based on their job function. If a user no longer requires access, SCIM updates Kubernetes policies to reflect the change, reducing the risk of privilege creep.

DevSecOps, an extension of DevOps that integrates security into every stage of the software development lifecycle, benefits from SCIM's automation capabilities. Security policies must adapt to dynamic development environments where identities change frequently. SCIM ensures that security policies remain up to date by synchronizing identity attributes with security tools such as vulnerability scanners, code analysis platforms, and incident response systems. If a developer is assigned to a high-security project, SCIM can enforce additional authentication requirements and monitoring controls automatically.

Logging and auditing are essential in DevOps environments to track identity changes and access patterns. SCIM enables organizations to maintain detailed logs of user provisioning, updates, and deprovisioning events across all CI/CD tools. These logs help security teams identify unauthorized access attempts, enforce compliance with regulatory requirements, and investigate incidents. SCIM-integrated logging solutions can aggregate identity events into centralized monitoring platforms such as Splunk, ELK Stack, or Azure Monitor, providing real-time visibility into identity management activities.

SCIM's support for schema extensions allows organizations to define custom identity attributes that align with DevOps workflows. While SCIM provides standard attributes for user profiles, organizations may require additional attributes such as GitHub repository access levels, CI/CD pipeline permissions, or infrastructure deployment rights. SCIM schema extensions enable these attributes to be synchronized across all tools, ensuring that access policies remain consistent and transparent.

Performance optimization is critical in fast-paced DevOps environments where identity synchronization must occur in real time. SCIM supports filtering, pagination, and incremental updates to ensure efficient identity synchronization without overloading CI/CD systems. Instead of retrieving all user records, SCIM allows DevOps tools to request only relevant updates based on recent changes. This reduces API overhead and ensures that identity updates propagate quickly across distributed development environments.

SCIM also simplifies onboarding and offboarding processes for DevOps teams. When a new developer joins a project, SCIM provisions their accounts in all required tools, ensuring that they can start contributing immediately. If a developer transitions to a different project, SCIM updates their access permissions accordingly, preventing unnecessary delays. Automated onboarding and offboarding reduce administrative overhead, allowing DevOps teams to focus on innovation rather than manual identity management.

SCIM's ability to integrate with DevOps pipelines, cloud platforms, and security tools makes it an essential component of modern CI/CD environments. Organizations that implement SCIM in their DevOps workflows benefit from improved automation, enhanced security, and streamlined access control. SCIM ensures that developer identities remain synchronized across all tools and services, enabling organizations to scale their DevOps practices without compromising security or operational efficiency.

SCIM and Zero Trust Security

SCIM plays a vital role in Zero Trust Security by automating identity lifecycle management, enforcing least privilege access, and ensuring real-time synchronization of user attributes across multiple security systems. Zero Trust is a modern security framework that assumes no user, device, or system should be inherently trusted, requiring continuous authentication and authorization based on real-time identity data. SCIM integrates with Zero Trust architectures by providing a standardized approach to provisioning, updating, and deprovisioning user identities across cloud, on-premises, and hybrid environments.

Zero Trust Security relies on strong identity and access management (IAM) to enforce strict authentication and authorization policies. Traditional perimeter-based security models grant broad access based on network location, assuming that internal users can be trusted. Zero Trust eliminates this assumption by requiring users and devices to continuously prove their identity and security posture before accessing resources. SCIM enhances this model by ensuring that identity attributes such as roles, group memberships, and security policies remain updated across all security controls, preventing outdated access permissions from being exploited.

Identity provisioning is a critical component of Zero Trust, ensuring that users have only the minimum required access to perform their tasks. SCIM automates this process by provisioning user accounts across all necessary applications and security systems as soon as they are onboarded. When a new employee joins an organization, SCIM synchronizes their identity with identity providers, multi-factor authentication (MFA) systems, endpoint security solutions, and Zero Trust access gateways. This automation reduces the risk of misconfigurations and ensures that access policies align with the principle of least privilege.

SCIM also facilitates dynamic access control by integrating with Zero Trust policy engines. Many organizations use policy-based access control (PBAC) or attribute-based access control (ABAC) to enforce security policies based on user attributes. SCIM synchronizes these attributes, such as department, job function, security clearance, and risk level, across all applications and security platforms. If a user's risk score changes due to suspicious activity, SCIM ensures that security tools receive this update in real time, triggering adaptive security measures such as step-up authentication or restricted access.

User deprovisioning is a key security requirement in Zero Trust environments, preventing unauthorized access when employees leave an organization or change roles. SCIM automates this process by ensuring that user accounts are disabled or removed from all connected applications immediately upon termination. Traditional security models often fail to revoke access promptly, leaving orphaned accounts that attackers can exploit. SCIM eliminates this risk by propagating deprovisioning requests to all integrated systems, ensuring that users no longer have access to corporate resources.

Multi-factor authentication (MFA) is a fundamental requirement in Zero Trust architectures, providing an additional layer of security beyond passwords. SCIM ensures that MFA-related attributes, such as enrolled authentication devices, biometric registrations, and phone numbers, are consistently updated across all authentication services. This synchronization prevents authentication failures caused by outdated security attributes and ensures that users can securely access resources with their registered authentication factors. If a user loses their MFA device, SCIM updates their authentication records, allowing a smooth transition to a new security method without disrupting access.

Zero Trust Security extends beyond user identities to include device identities, ensuring that only trusted devices can access corporate resources. SCIM plays a role in device identity management by synchronizing device attributes such as ownership, security posture, and compliance status across endpoint security solutions. Organizations implementing Zero Trust Network Access (ZTNA) rely on real-time device data to make access decisions. SCIM ensures that if a device falls out of compliance, security policies are enforced immediately, restricting access to sensitive data and applications.

SCIM enhances Zero Trust Security by enabling continuous monitoring and auditing of identity changes. Security teams need visibility into identity modifications, access requests, and authentication events to detect anomalies and potential security threats. SCIM integrates with security information and event management (SIEM) systems, logging identity changes in real time. These logs help security analysts detect suspicious activity, such as unauthorized privilege escalations, unexpected group membership changes, or failed deprovisioning attempts. By maintaining a detailed audit trail, SCIM supports regulatory compliance requirements and security investigations.

Zero Trust policies require granular control over access based on user behavior, location, and risk levels. SCIM integrates with risk-based authentication systems, ensuring that user attributes such as login patterns, device fingerprints, and geolocation data are updated dynamically. If a user attempts to access a resource from an unusual location or exhibits behavior that deviates from their normal activity, SCIM ensures that security policies are adjusted accordingly. This enables organizations to enforce dynamic access restrictions without disrupting legitimate users.

SCIM also supports just-in-time (JIT) provisioning in Zero Trust environments, allowing temporary access to resources based on real-time security assessments. Organizations often require contractors, vendors, or temporary employees to access specific applications for limited periods. SCIM enables automated provisioning workflows that grant time-limited access based on predefined policies. Once the access period expires, SCIM automatically deprovisions the user, preventing unauthorized access beyond the required timeframe. This approach reduces the risk of excessive privileges and improves security governance.

Security automation is a core principle of Zero Trust, ensuring that identity-related changes are applied instantly across all systems. SCIM enables automated enforcement of security policies by synchronizing identity attributes with security orchestration and automation platforms. If a security event, such as a credential compromise, is detected, SCIM ensures that access permissions are revoked or modified in real time. This automation reduces the attack surface by minimizing the window of opportunity for malicious actors to exploit compromised credentials.

Hybrid and multi-cloud environments require consistent identity synchronization across multiple identity providers, cloud services, and on-premises directories. SCIM ensures that Zero Trust policies remain effective by maintaining identity consistency across these diverse environments. Organizations using Microsoft Entra ID, Okta, Google Workspace, and on-premises Active Directory can rely on SCIM to unify identity management, preventing gaps in security enforcement. SCIM also enables organizations to extend Zero Trust policies to third-party SaaS applications by synchronizing user identities with cloud-based access control solutions.

SCIM schema extensions allow organizations to define additional identity attributes specific to their Zero Trust implementations. While SCIM provides standard attributes such as userName, emails, and groups, organizations may require attributes related to security policies, access levels, or compliance certifications. SCIM schema extensions enable the synchronization of these attributes across security platforms, ensuring that Zero Trust policies are enforced based on comprehensive identity data. Organizations can define attributes such as securityClearanceLevel, riskScore, and authenticationStrength to refine access control decisions.

Performance optimization is crucial in Zero Trust environments, where real-time identity synchronization is required to enforce security policies. SCIM supports filtering, pagination, and incremental updates to ensure efficient data synchronization. Instead of retrieving all user records, SCIM allows security systems to request only the necessary updates, reducing API load and improving response times. These optimizations enable organizations to scale their Zero Trust architectures without compromising performance.

SCIM ensures that Zero Trust Security remains effective by providing a unified, automated, and scalable approach to identity synchronization. Organizations implementing Zero Trust rely on SCIM to maintain accurate identity attributes, enforce least privilege access, and integrate with security monitoring and enforcement tools. SCIM's ability to automate user provisioning, deprovisioning, and real-time identity updates strengthens Zero Trust frameworks, reducing security risks while improving operational efficiency.

SCIM for Workforce Identity Management

SCIM plays a critical role in workforce identity management by automating user provisioning, synchronization, and deprovisioning across enterprise applications. Managing workforce identities efficiently is essential for ensuring secure access to company resources while reducing administrative overhead. Organizations must maintain accurate identity records for employees, contractors, and partners across multiple applications and services. SCIM provides a standardized approach to workforce identity management, ensuring that user attributes remain consistent, access is granted and revoked appropriately, and compliance requirements are met.

Enterprises rely on identity providers to manage workforce identities centrally. These identity providers, such as Microsoft Entra ID, Okta, and Google Workspace, store user attributes, authentication policies, and access permissions. Without SCIM, integrating identity providers with applications requires custom connectors or manual updates, leading to delays, errors, and security risks. SCIM simplifies this integration by allowing identity providers to communicate with applications using a common REST-based API, ensuring that workforce identity data is synchronized automatically.

User provisioning is a fundamental aspect of workforce identity management. When a new employee joins an organization, their identity must be created in various applications, including collaboration tools, email platforms, HR systems, and security services. SCIM automates this process by provisioning user accounts as soon as they are created in the identity provider. Instead of manually creating accounts in each application, organizations use SCIM to ensure that new employees receive immediate access to the tools they need based on their role, department, and business requirements.

SCIM ensures that user attributes remain consistent across all connected applications. Workforce identities include attributes such as userName, email, givenName, familyName, jobTitle, department, and manager. These attributes must be updated dynamically when employees change roles, transfer to new departments, or update their contact information. SCIM synchronizes these changes in real time, preventing inconsistencies where outdated user attributes could cause access issues or misconfigured permissions.

Role-based access control (RBAC) is a common approach in workforce identity management, ensuring that users receive appropriate access based on their job function. SCIM integrates with RBAC systems by synchronizing user roles and group memberships across all enterprise applications. If an organization defines access policies based on groups such as "Finance Team" or "IT Administrators," SCIM ensures that users are automatically assigned to or removed from these groups based on their role changes. This automation reduces the risk of privilege escalation and enforces least privilege access across the workforce.

Contractors, temporary workers, and external partners also require access to enterprise applications, but their identities must be managed with stricter controls. SCIM ensures that non-employee workforce identities are provisioned with appropriate access levels and deprovisioned when their contracts end. Many organizations implement SCIM workflows that automatically revoke access for contractors after a predefined period, reducing the risk of unauthorized access. If an external consultant requires extended access, SCIM updates their identity attributes to reflect the new contract terms, ensuring compliance with security policies.

User deprovisioning is a critical function in workforce identity management. When an employee leaves the organization, their access must be revoked across all applications to prevent security risks associated with orphaned accounts. SCIM automates the deprovisioning process by detecting when a user is disabled or deleted in the identity provider and propagating this change to all connected applications. This prevents former employees from retaining access to corporate data and reduces the risk of account misuse.

Security policies in workforce identity management often include multi-factor authentication (MFA), device trust requirements, and session management rules. SCIM ensures that authentication-related attributes, such as phone numbers for SMS-based authentication or registered authentication devices, remain synchronized across all security systems. If an employee registers a new authentication device, SCIM updates this information in all connected applications, preventing authentication failures caused by outdated security attributes.

Enterprises must comply with industry regulations such as GDPR, HIPAA, and SOC 2, which require strict identity governance practices. SCIM supports compliance by maintaining audit logs of all identity changes, including provisioning, role updates, and deprovisioning events. Security teams use these logs to track user access, detect unauthorized changes, and enforce regulatory policies. SCIM-integrated identity governance solutions enable organizations to generate reports on workforce identity management, demonstrating compliance with security and privacy regulations.

Hybrid and multi-cloud environments require consistent workforce identity synchronization across different platforms. Many organizations operate a mix of on-premises identity systems, such as Active Directory, and cloud-based identity providers. SCIM enables seamless synchronization between these systems, ensuring that workforce identities remain updated regardless of where authentication occurs. This eliminates the complexity of managing separate identity silos and ensures a unified approach to workforce identity management.

Performance optimization is essential in large enterprises where thousands or millions of workforce identities must be synchronized efficiently. SCIM supports filtering, pagination, and incremental updates to ensure that identity synchronization processes do not overload system resources. Instead of retrieving all user records, SCIM allows applications to request only relevant updates, improving API efficiency and reducing network bandwidth usage. Organizations using SCIM for workforce identity management benefit from real-time identity updates without unnecessary data transfers.

SCIM also enhances just-in-time (JIT) provisioning for workforce identity management, allowing applications to create user accounts dynamically when an employee logs in for the first time. While JIT provisioning reduces the need for pre-created accounts, it does not handle attribute updates or deprovisioning effectively. SCIM complements JIT provisioning by ensuring that workforce identities remain synchronized continuously and that accounts are removed when no longer needed. This prevents identity drift, where outdated user information leads to access control failures.

Workforce identity management often involves integration with HR systems, which serve as the authoritative source for employee records. SCIM enables seamless integration between HR platforms and identity providers, ensuring that identity updates from HR systems propagate to all connected applications. If an employee's job title or department is updated in the HR system, SCIM ensures that this change is reflected in access control policies, preventing mismatches between workforce roles and assigned permissions.

SCIM schema extensions allow organizations to define additional workforce identity attributes that are specific to their business needs. While SCIM provides a standard schema for user attributes, enterprises may require custom attributes such as employeeType, securityClearance, or projectAssignment. SCIM schema extensions enable these attributes to be synchronized across all applications, ensuring that workforce identity policies remain aligned with business requirements. By defining custom schemas, organizations maintain flexibility in their identity management strategy while adhering to SCIM standards.

SCIM enhances workforce identity management by providing a scalable, automated, and secure approach to user provisioning and synchronization. Organizations that implement SCIM benefit from improved operational efficiency, reduced security risks, and seamless integration with identity providers and workforce applications. SCIM ensures that workforce identities remain consistent, access permissions are enforced dynamically, and identity governance policies are maintained across all enterprise systems.

SCIM for Customer Identity Management

SCIM provides a scalable and standardized approach to customer identity management by automating the provisioning, synchronization, and deprovisioning of customer accounts across multiple applications and services. Organizations that manage large customer bases need efficient identity solutions that ensure accurate user data, seamless authentication, and enhanced security. SCIM simplifies customer identity management by integrating identity providers with customer-facing applications, reducing administrative overhead, improving user experience, and maintaining data consistency across systems.

Customer identity management differs from workforce identity management because it involves external users who interact with a company's services rather than employees accessing internal resources. Customers expect a seamless and secure experience when registering, updating their profiles, or accessing services. SCIM enables organizations to manage customer identities dynamically, ensuring that user profiles remain synchronized across all applications, including web portals, mobile apps, and cloud-based services. Instead of requiring manual updates, SCIM automatically propagates identity changes, reducing friction and improving customer satisfaction.

User registration is a critical component of customer identity management. When a new customer signs up for a service, their identity must be created across various backend systems, including authentication platforms, customer relationship management (CRM) tools, and analytics platforms. SCIM automates this process by provisioning customer accounts across all integrated services upon registration. Whether a customer registers through a website, mobile app, or third-party authentication provider, SCIM ensures that their profile is consistently created and updated in all connected systems.

Profile synchronization is essential for maintaining accurate customer data. Customers frequently update their information, including email addresses, phone numbers, and preferences. Without SCIM, these updates may not propagate to all applications, leading to inconsistencies and potential service disruptions. SCIM ensures that profile changes made in one system are automatically reflected in all connected services. If a customer updates their email address in a self-service portal, SCIM ensures that authentication systems, marketing platforms, and billing systems receive the updated information in real time.

Authentication and authorization in customer identity management often rely on external identity providers such as Google, Facebook, Apple, and enterprise single sign-on (SSO) solutions. SCIM integrates with these identity providers to ensure that customer identities are provisioned and updated correctly. When a customer logs in using an external identity provider, SCIM synchronizes their attributes with backend applications, ensuring that access permissions and profile data remain consistent. This integration allows businesses to offer flexible authentication options while maintaining centralized identity management.

Customer segmentation and personalized experiences depend on accurate identity data. Organizations use customer attributes such as location, purchase history, and subscription status to tailor content and offers. SCIM ensures that these attributes remain synchronized across personalization engines, recommendation systems, and customer support platforms. If a customer upgrades their subscription, SCIM updates their profile in all relevant applications, ensuring that they immediately receive premium features and services. This real-time synchronization enhances customer engagement and retention.

SCIM supports group-based and attribute-based access control for customer identities. Many online services offer tiered memberships, loyalty programs, or enterprise subscriptions with different levels of access. SCIM automates the assignment of customer groups based on their subscription plan or account type. If a customer upgrades from a free to a paid plan, SCIM updates their access rights across all applications, granting them the appropriate permissions without requiring manual intervention. This automation simplifies customer lifecycle management and ensures that users always have the correct access level.

Security and compliance are critical in customer identity management, especially for organizations handling sensitive user data. Regulations such as GDPR, CCPA, and PCI-DSS require businesses to protect customer information and enforce strict access controls. SCIM supports compliance by ensuring that customer identity records are managed securely and that access to personal data is restricted based on predefined policies. SCIM also maintains audit logs of identity changes, allowing organizations to track customer account modifications and ensure regulatory compliance.

User deprovisioning is an essential security measure for protecting customer accounts. Customers may deactivate their accounts, unsubscribe from services, or request data deletion under privacy regulations. SCIM automates the deprovisioning process by ensuring that customer accounts are removed or anonymized across all connected applications. If a customer deletes their account, SCIM propagates this action to authentication providers, analytics platforms, and CRM systems, ensuring that no residual personal data remains. This capability supports privacy compliance and reduces the risk of unauthorized access to inactive accounts.

Multi-factor authentication (MFA) is increasingly required for customer accounts to enhance security. SCIM ensures that MFA-related attributes, such as phone numbers, registered devices, and authentication preferences, are consistently updated across authentication systems. If a customer enrolls in MFA or changes their authentication method, SCIM ensures that this update is reflected in all connected applications. This synchronization prevents authentication failures caused by outdated security attributes and improves the overall security posture of customer identity management systems.

Organizations operating in multi-cloud environments must synchronize customer identities across multiple platforms, including public clouds, private data centers, and third-party applications. SCIM enables seamless identity synchronization across these diverse environments, ensuring that customer profiles remain consistent regardless of where authentication occurs. If a customer signs in through a cloud-based identity provider, SCIM ensures that their profile updates are applied to all connected applications, eliminating identity silos and enhancing user experience.

Performance optimization is essential for customer identity management, where real-time synchronization of user profiles is required. SCIM supports incremental updates, filtering, and pagination to ensure efficient identity synchronization without overloading backend systems. Instead of synchronizing all customer accounts at once, SCIM allows applications to request only the necessary updates, improving API efficiency and reducing latency. This approach ensures that identity updates are processed quickly, enabling responsive and scalable customer identity management solutions.

SCIM schema extensions allow organizations to define custom attributes for customer identities. While SCIM provides a standard schema for user profiles, businesses often require additional attributes such as loyalty points, purchase history, or communication preferences. SCIM schema extensions enable these attributes to be synchronized across all connected applications, ensuring that customer identity records remain comprehensive and up to date. Organizations can define custom schemas that align with their business needs while maintaining interoperability with SCIM-compliant identity providers.

Customer self-service portals benefit from SCIM by enabling users to manage their own identity attributes without administrative intervention. When a customer updates their profile, SCIM propagates these changes to all connected applications automatically. This reduces support requests and improves user satisfaction by ensuring that changes take effect immediately across all services. Self-service capabilities combined with SCIM-driven automation enhance the efficiency of customer identity management.

SCIM enhances customer identity management by providing a standardized, automated, and secure approach to identity provisioning and synchronization. Organizations that implement SCIM benefit from improved customer experience, reduced administrative burden, and stronger security controls. SCIM ensures that customer identities remain consistent across all applications, supporting seamless authentication, access management, and compliance with data privacy regulations.

SCIM and Compliance (GDPR, CCPA, etc.)

SCIM plays a crucial role in regulatory compliance by automating identity lifecycle management and ensuring accurate user data across multiple systems. Regulations such as the General Data Protection Regulation (GDPR), the California Consumer Privacy Act (CCPA), and other data protection laws require organizations to enforce strict identity governance policies, protect personal data, and maintain transparency in data processing. SCIM provides a standardized approach to user provisioning, updates, and deprovisioning, ensuring that compliance requirements are met while reducing administrative overhead.

GDPR mandates that organizations protect the personal data of individuals within the European Union. This includes ensuring that personal data is processed lawfully, kept accurate, and deleted when no longer necessary. SCIM enables organizations to comply with GDPR by ensuring that identity attributes remain synchronized and that user data is updated or deleted across all connected applications. When a user requests data deletion under the "right to be forgotten," SCIM propagates this request to all systems, ensuring that no residual personal data remains in unauthorized locations.

CCPA grants California residents rights over their personal data, including the right to access, delete, and restrict data sharing. Organizations subject to CCPA must ensure that customer identity records remain consistent across all applications to facilitate compliance requests. SCIM automates these processes by ensuring that user data is updated, access is restricted when required, and deletion requests are enforced across multiple identity stores. If a customer requests to opt out of data sharing, SCIM ensures that this preference is reflected in marketing platforms, customer relationship management (CRM) systems, and other connected services.

Auditability and record-keeping are key compliance requirements under GDPR, CCPA, and similar regulations. Organizations must track identity-related changes, including user account creation, role modifications, and access revocations. SCIM supports compliance by maintaining detailed logs of identity events, allowing organizations to generate audit reports and demonstrate compliance with regulatory requirements. Security teams use these logs to track data access patterns, detect unauthorized changes, and enforce policies that prevent identity misuse.

Access control and data minimization are fundamental principles of compliance. GDPR and other regulations require that organizations limit access to personal data based on necessity. SCIM enforces these principles by integrating with role-based access control (RBAC) and attribute-based access control (ABAC) systems. By ensuring that user roles and attributes remain updated in all applications, SCIM prevents excessive permissions and enforces least privilege access. If an employee changes roles, SCIM automatically adjusts their access rights, ensuring that they can only access data relevant to their new responsibilities.

Consent management is another critical aspect of compliance, particularly for regulations that require explicit user consent before processing personal data. SCIM ensures that consent-related attributes, such as opt-in preferences and data-sharing consents, are synchronized across all applications. If a user withdraws consent, SCIM ensures that all systems respect this change, preventing further data processing without authorization. This automation reduces the risk of compliance violations caused by outdated or inconsistent consent records.

Data portability is a requirement under GDPR, giving users the right to obtain and transfer their personal data between service providers. SCIM facilitates data portability by standardizing user identity records and enabling seamless data transfers between identity providers. When a user requests their data, SCIM ensures that their identity attributes are retrieved and exported in a structured, machine-readable format. This simplifies the process of fulfilling data portability requests while maintaining data integrity.

Third-party risk management is essential for organizations that rely on external service providers to process identity data. Regulations require organizations to ensure that third-party vendors comply with data protection standards. SCIM reduces third-party risk by enforcing standardized identity synchronization, ensuring that external applications only receive authorized identity attributes. By automating user provisioning and deprovisioning, SCIM minimizes the risk of unauthorized data access by third-party vendors.

Breach notification requirements under GDPR and CCPA mandate that organizations detect and report data breaches within a specified timeframe. SCIM enhances security monitoring by integrating with security information and event management (SIEM) systems, ensuring that identity-related anomalies are detected in real time. If an unauthorized identity change is detected, SCIM enables security teams to respond quickly, limiting the impact of potential data breaches and ensuring compliance with reporting obligations.

SCIM also improves compliance with industry-specific regulations such as HIPAA for healthcare data protection and SOC 2 for security and privacy controls in cloud services. Healthcare organizations must ensure that patient identity records remain secure and that access is granted only to authorized individuals. SCIM enforces HIPAA compliance by synchronizing identity attributes with electronic health record (EHR) systems, ensuring that only approved users can access sensitive health information. Similarly, SOC 2 compliance requires strong identity governance practices, which SCIM facilitates by automating identity management and maintaining access logs.

Employee data protection regulations also require strict control over workforce identities. Many labor laws mandate that employee records be managed securely, with access restricted based on employment status. SCIM ensures compliance with these regulations by synchronizing employee identity attributes across human resources (HR) systems, payroll platforms, and access management tools. If an employee leaves the organization, SCIM ensures that their identity records are deactivated, preventing unauthorized access to corporate systems.

Encryption and data security requirements under GDPR and other regulations require that personal data be protected against unauthorized access. SCIM integrates with encryption and tokenization platforms to ensure that identity attributes are transmitted and stored securely. By enforcing encryption standards across identity synchronization processes, SCIM helps organizations comply with data protection laws that mandate the secure handling of personal information.

SCIM supports regulatory reporting and compliance assessments by enabling organizations to generate real-time identity management reports. Compliance teams use SCIM-driven reporting tools to track identity modifications, monitor access control enforcement, and verify data protection measures. These reports help organizations prepare for regulatory audits, ensuring that identity governance policies align with legal and industry standards.

Cross-border data transfer regulations require organizations to manage identity data in compliance with regional data protection laws. Many regulations restrict the transfer of personal data outside specific geographic regions unless adequate protections are in place. SCIM enables organizations to enforce data residency policies by synchronizing identity attributes within compliant cloud regions. By ensuring that personal data is processed according to regulatory requirements, SCIM helps organizations mitigate legal risks associated with international data transfers.

Organizations that implement SCIM as part of their compliance strategy benefit from automated identity governance, improved data security, and reduced regulatory risk. SCIM ensures that user identities remain accurate, access permissions align with compliance policies, and personal data is managed according to legal requirements. By integrating SCIM with identity providers, security tools, and compliance frameworks, organizations create a scalable and secure approach to regulatory compliance in identity management.

SCIM Performance and Scalability

SCIM is designed to provide efficient, scalable, and high-performance identity synchronization across cloud, hybrid, and on-premises environments. As organizations grow and manage thousands or even millions of user identities across multiple systems, the performance of SCIM implementations becomes critical. A well-optimized SCIM deployment ensures that user provisioning, updates, and deprovisioning operations happen in real-time without overwhelming system resources. Scalability is essential for enterprises that need to support dynamic identity synchronization across a large number of applications, identity providers, and service providers.

SCIM operates using RESTful APIs, enabling lightweight and efficient communication between identity providers and service providers. The design of these APIs plays a crucial role in performance optimization. SCIM endpoints must be capable of handling high-frequency API calls, especially in environments where identity updates occur frequently. Rate limiting and API throttling are commonly used to prevent excessive requests from overloading SCIM servers while ensuring that identity synchronization remains responsive. Organizations implementing SCIM should configure appropriate rate limits to balance performance and availability.

Pagination is a key performance feature in SCIM, allowing clients to request large sets of user data in smaller, manageable chunks. Instead of retrieving an entire user directory at once, SCIM enables clients to use the startIndex and count parameters to paginate results. This improves API efficiency by reducing memory usage and processing overhead, particularly when dealing with large-scale identity synchronization. Well-designed SCIM implementations optimize pagination queries to ensure minimal latency and efficient data retrieval.

Filtering enhances SCIM performance by enabling clients to request only the relevant subset of identity data rather than fetching all records. The SCIM filter parameter allows identity providers and service providers to refine queries based on attributes such as userName, email, department, or active status. By narrowing the scope of API requests, filtering reduces unnecessary data transfers and speeds up synchronization processes. For example, an identity provider might request only active users in a specific department rather than retrieving all users in the system.

Incremental updates further improve SCIM scalability by synchronizing only modified records instead of processing full identity lists repeatedly. SCIM supports timestamp-based synchronization, where clients request changes since the last update using attributes such as meta.lastModified. This ensures that only users who have been created, updated, or deleted are processed, significantly reducing API load and improving response times. Implementing incremental updates prevents redundant operations and minimizes the performance impact on both identity providers and service providers.

SCIM servers must be designed to handle concurrent requests efficiently, ensuring that multiple identity synchronization operations can occur in parallel. Load balancing distributes incoming SCIM API requests across multiple SCIM servers, preventing bottlenecks and ensuring high availability. Horizontal scaling, where additional SCIM server instances are added as demand increases, is an effective approach for managing large-scale identity synchronization. Organizations deploying SCIM in cloud environments can use auto-scaling features to dynamically adjust resources based on API request volume.

Caching mechanisms enhance SCIM performance by reducing the need for repeated database queries. SCIM implementations often cache frequently accessed user attributes and query results to speed up API responses. Proper cache expiration policies ensure that data remains accurate while minimizing performance overhead. In high-traffic environments, distributed caching solutions such as Redis or Memcached help SCIM servers process identity requests faster without overwhelming backend databases.

Asynchronous processing improves SCIM scalability by decoupling identity synchronization tasks from real-time API requests. Instead of processing all identity updates synchronously, SCIM implementations can use message queues or event-driven architectures to handle provisioning and deprovisioning operations asynchronously. This approach prevents delays in API responses while ensuring that identity changes are applied consistently across all connected systems. Asynchronous workflows are particularly useful in large-scale deployments where real-time processing of every identity event may introduce unnecessary latency.

Service providers integrating SCIM must ensure that their SCIM endpoints are optimized for high availability and fault tolerance. Redundancy and failover mechanisms help maintain SCIM service continuity in case of server failures or network disruptions. Deploying SCIM services across multiple geographic regions further enhances scalability by distributing identity synchronization tasks closer to end users, reducing network latency and improving overall performance.

Security and performance optimizations must be balanced to ensure that SCIM requests are processed efficiently without compromising identity data protection. SCIM supports authentication and authorization through OAuth 2.0, requiring API tokens to be validated before processing requests. Token validation mechanisms must be optimized to prevent authentication overhead while maintaining security best practices. Using lightweight JWT-based authentication reduces token validation latency compared to database-backed session management.

SCIM schema design also influences performance, as overly complex schemas with excessive attributes may lead to slower API responses. Organizations implementing SCIM should define schemas that include only necessary attributes while leveraging schema extensions for specific use cases. Optimizing attribute selection ensures that SCIM requests retrieve only relevant data, reducing API processing time and improving scalability.

Event-driven SCIM synchronization enhances performance by triggering updates based on real-time changes rather than relying on periodic bulk synchronization jobs. Many identity providers and service providers implement webhook-based SCIM integrations, where updates are pushed to SCIM endpoints as soon as identity changes occur. This approach reduces unnecessary polling, improves data freshness, and minimizes the computational load associated with scheduled synchronization tasks.

Monitoring and performance analytics are essential for maintaining scalable SCIM deployments. Organizations should track API response times, request rates, error rates, and synchronization latency to identify performance bottlenecks. Logging SCIM operations enables administrators to troubleshoot issues and optimize query execution.

Integrating SCIM with observability tools such as Prometheus, Grafana, or ELK Stack helps organizations monitor identity synchronization performance in real-time.

Testing and performance benchmarking ensure that SCIM implementations meet scalability requirements before deployment. Organizations should conduct load testing to simulate high API request volumes and evaluate how SCIM services handle concurrent synchronization tasks. Identifying performance bottlenecks early allows for infrastructure optimizations such as database indexing, API rate limiting, and horizontal scaling.

SCIM's ability to handle large-scale identity synchronization depends on well-architected infrastructure, optimized API implementations, and strategic use of caching, filtering, and incremental updates. Organizations that implement SCIM with performance and scalability in mind benefit from faster identity provisioning, reduced synchronization latency, and efficient resource utilization. SCIM ensures that identity data remains accurate and up to date across all connected applications, supporting seamless user experiences and security compliance.

SCIM Security Best Practices

SCIM is a powerful identity management protocol that automates user provisioning, synchronization, and deprovisioning across multiple applications. Securing SCIM implementations is critical to ensuring the confidentiality, integrity, and availability of identity data. Organizations using SCIM must enforce strict security controls to protect user identities from unauthorized access, data breaches, and privilege escalation. Implementing security best practices ensures that SCIM remains a reliable and secure method for managing identity information across cloud, hybrid, and on-premises environments.

Authentication and authorization are fundamental components of SCIM security. SCIM APIs should always require strong authentication mechanisms to prevent unauthorized access. OAuth 2.0 is the preferred authentication framework for SCIM, allowing identity providers and service providers to issue access tokens that authenticate API requests. Tokens must be securely managed, with short expiration times and rotation policies to reduce the risk of misuse. Implementing mutual TLS (mTLS) enhances security by requiring client certificates for authentication, ensuring that only trusted clients can access SCIM endpoints.

Least privilege access should be enforced to minimize security risks associated with excessive permissions. SCIM clients should be granted only the permissions necessary to perform their designated operations. OAuth 2.0 scopes should be used to define fine-grained access control, ensuring that clients can only read, write, or delete user identities based on their assigned permissions. Service providers must validate scopes before processing SCIM requests, preventing unauthorized modifications to identity data.

SCIM endpoints must be protected against common web security vulnerabilities. Input validation is essential to prevent injection attacks, including SQL injection and XML external entity (XXE) attacks. All user inputs should be sanitized, and API requests should be validated against predefined schemas to ensure they conform to expected formats. Rate limiting and API throttling prevent abuse by restricting the number of requests a client can make within a given timeframe. These controls help mitigate denial-of-service (DoS) attacks and unauthorized data scraping.

Data encryption protects identity information during transmission and storage. SCIM APIs should enforce HTTPS with TLS 1.2 or higher to secure data in transit. Weak cipher suites should be disabled to prevent cryptographic attacks. Sensitive identity attributes, such as passwords, security questions, and authentication tokens, should be encrypted at rest using strong encryption algorithms such as AES-256. Role-based encryption ensures that only authorized entities can decrypt and access specific identity attributes.

Logging and auditing provide visibility into SCIM operations, enabling security teams to detect and investigate suspicious activity. All SCIM requests, including provisioning, modifications, and deprovisioning events, should be logged with relevant metadata, such as timestamps, client identifiers, and user details. Logs should be centralized and monitored in real time to identify anomalies, failed authentication attempts, and unauthorized API calls. Security information and event management (SIEM) solutions can be integrated with SCIM logs to trigger alerts based on predefined security policies.

Token security is essential for protecting SCIM authentication mechanisms. OAuth 2.0 access tokens should have limited lifespans to reduce the risk of token theft and misuse. Refresh tokens should be used cautiously, with strict expiration policies and client validation to prevent unauthorized access. JWT (JSON Web Token) signatures should be validated to ensure that tokens have not been tampered with. Revocation mechanisms should be implemented to invalidate tokens when users are deprovisioned or when access needs to be restricted.

SCIM clients and servers should implement secure coding practices to prevent vulnerabilities. Secure coding frameworks should be followed to avoid buffer overflows, improper error handling, and insecure deserialization. API responses should provide minimal error details to prevent information disclosure. Security headers, such as Content-Security-Policy and Strict-Transport-Security, should be enforced to protect against cross-site scripting (XSS) and man-in-the-middle (MITM) attacks.

User deprovisioning must be handled securely to prevent unauthorized access after account termination. SCIM should ensure that when users are deactivated in the identity provider, their access is revoked across all connected applications. Delayed or incomplete deprovisioning increases the risk of dormant accounts being exploited. Service providers should verify deprovisioning requests and confirm that all related resources, including API keys and session tokens, are revoked upon account removal.

Role-based access control (RBAC) and attribute-based access control (ABAC) should be implemented to enforce granular security policies. SCIM should synchronize user roles and attributes with access management systems to ensure that permissions align with security policies. If a user's role changes, SCIM should update access rights across all applications to prevent privilege escalation. Dynamic access controls based on user risk scores and device trust levels enhance security by adapting permissions in real time.

Multi-factor authentication (MFA) should be enforced for SCIM client authentication to reduce the risk of credential-based attacks. Organizations should require SCIM clients to authenticate using a combination of strong credentials and additional authentication factors. Hardware security modules (HSMs) and hardware tokens can be used to secure API keys and client credentials. Implementing adaptive authentication policies based on user behavior further enhances SCIM security.

Denial-of-service (DoS) and distributed denial-of-service (DDoS) attacks can disrupt SCIM services by overwhelming API endpoints with excessive requests. Web application firewalls (WAFs) and DDoS protection services should be deployed to filter malicious traffic. Rate limiting, IP whitelisting, and anomaly detection help prevent abuse by identifying and blocking suspicious request patterns. API gateways can be used to enforce traffic control policies and distribute load across multiple SCIM server instances.

Compliance with industry standards strengthens SCIM security by aligning with established security frameworks. Organizations should ensure that SCIM implementations comply with regulations such as GDPR, CCPA, HIPAA, and SOC 2. Compliance measures include implementing data minimization, enforcing access controls, and maintaining audit trails. Regular security assessments, penetration testing, and vulnerability scans should be conducted to identify and remediate security gaps.

API versioning and lifecycle management prevent security issues caused by deprecated SCIM endpoints. Organizations should establish clear versioning policies to ensure that SCIM clients use secure and supported API versions. Deprecation notices should be communicated in advance to allow clients to migrate to newer versions without disrupting identity synchronization. Secure API lifecycle management ensures that legacy endpoints do not expose vulnerabilities that could be exploited by attackers.

SCIM implementations should be regularly updated with security patches to address newly discovered vulnerabilities. Organizations should adopt a proactive approach to patch management, ensuring that SCIM servers, identity providers, and integrated applications remain protected against emerging threats. Automated security testing and continuous integration/continuous deployment (CI/CD) pipelines can be used to verify security updates before deploying them to production environments.

Regular security training and awareness programs should be provided to teams managing SCIM implementations. Security best practices should be embedded into development workflows, ensuring that developers, administrators, and security teams understand potential threats and mitigation strategies. Security policies should be documented and enforced through automated compliance checks, reducing the likelihood of misconfigurations that could expose identity data.

Organizations that implement SCIM security best practices benefit from stronger identity protection, reduced risk of unauthorized access, and improved compliance with regulatory requirements. SCIM enhances identity management security by ensuring that authentication, authorization, and data protection mechanisms are consistently enforced across all integrated applications. By adopting robust security measures, organizations can maintain a secure SCIM implementation while supporting scalable and efficient identity synchronization.

Troubleshooting SCIM Implementations

SCIM provides a standardized approach to identity provisioning and synchronization, but like any system, its implementation can encounter various challenges. Troubleshooting SCIM involves identifying and resolving issues related to authentication, authorization, API performance, data consistency, and integration with identity providers and service providers. Effective debugging techniques and structured problem-solving approaches are essential to maintaining a reliable SCIM deployment.

Authentication failures are one of the most common issues in SCIM implementations. SCIM relies on OAuth 2.0 for secure API authentication, and problems often arise when incorrect credentials, expired tokens, or misconfigured scopes are used. If SCIM API requests return 401 Unauthorized responses, administrators should verify that the client ID and client secret are correctly configured and that the access token is valid. Token introspection endpoints can be used to check token expiration and assigned scopes. If mutual TLS (mTLS) is used for authentication, certificate validation errors should be examined in server logs.

Authorization errors occur when SCIM clients attempt to perform actions beyond their allowed permissions. A 403 Forbidden response indicates that the client does not have the necessary scope to execute a specific operation. Identity providers should be configured to assign appropriate scopes, such as scim.read for retrieving user data or scim.write for modifying identities. SCIM server logs should be reviewed to determine whether role-based access control (RBAC) or attribute-based access control (ABAC) policies are preventing the request from succeeding.

Data consistency issues can arise when user attributes do not synchronize correctly between identity providers and service providers. If users appear with outdated information or missing attributes, SCIM filtering and attribute mapping should be examined. SCIM requests should include only relevant attributes using the attributes parameter to optimize data retrieval. Mismatched attribute names between identity providers and service providers often cause synchronization failures. Schema mapping should be verified to ensure that identity attributes such as userName, emails, and groups are correctly translated.

Provisioning failures may occur due to missing required attributes, schema mismatches, or validation errors. A 400 Bad Request response indicates that the SCIM request contains invalid data. API responses typically include error messages that provide details about missing fields or incorrect attribute formats. If a SCIM server enforces required attributes such as userName or emails, client applications must ensure that these attributes are always included in provisioning requests. Schema extensions should be reviewed to confirm that custom attributes are properly registered and used consistently across all systems.

Performance issues in SCIM implementations can lead to slow API responses, timeouts, or high server load. SCIM servers handling large identity directories should implement pagination using the startIndex and count parameters to retrieve manageable chunks of user data. Excessive full synchronization requests should be avoided in favor of incremental updates using meta.lastModified timestamps. Server-side caching can reduce the load on SCIM endpoints by minimizing repeated database queries for frequently accessed identity attributes.

Rate limiting and API throttling may cause intermittent failures in SCIM synchronization. Service providers often enforce rate limits to prevent abuse and ensure fair resource allocation. If a 429 Too Many Requests response is encountered, SCIM clients should implement retry mechanisms with exponential backoff to prevent excessive request bursts. Identity providers should be configured to distribute API calls evenly over time, reducing the likelihood of hitting rate limits. If rate limits are too restrictive, service providers may allow rate limit adjustments based on usage patterns.

SCIM bulk operations can introduce complexity when processing large identity updates. If bulk requests fail, reviewing error responses within the bulk operation payload is essential. SCIM servers may reject specific operations within a bulk request while processing others successfully. Identifying failed operations and retrying them individually can help isolate issues. Bulk requests should be optimized by limiting the number of operations per request to prevent excessive processing times and memory consumption.

User deprovisioning errors can result in orphaned accounts if SCIM DELETE requests fail. If a 404 Not Found response occurs, it may indicate that the user record no longer exists in the target system. If DELETE operations are not supported by a service provider, SCIM PATCH requests should be used to mark users as inactive instead. Ensuring that deprovisioning workflows are properly implemented prevents unauthorized access and reduces security risks associated with inactive accounts.

Integration issues between SCIM and identity providers often stem from configuration mismatches. Identity providers such as Microsoft Entra ID, Okta, and Google Workspace require SCIM endpoints to be configured correctly with the correct base URL, authentication method, and attribute mappings. If SCIM synchronization does not work as expected, reviewing the identity provider's logs and synchronization history can help identify configuration errors. API testing tools such as Postman or cURL can be used to manually send SCIM requests and verify responses.

Timeout errors may occur when SCIM servers take too long to process requests, especially in large-scale deployments. Increasing timeout thresholds on SCIM clients can mitigate issues caused by temporary network delays, but long response times often indicate underlying performance bottlenecks. Optimizing database queries, indexing frequently accessed identity attributes, and using asynchronous processing for provisioning tasks can improve SCIM server response times.

SCIM versioning conflicts can arise when service providers implement different SCIM specifications. Some applications may support SCIM 1.1 while others use SCIM 2.0, leading to compatibility issues. Ensuring that both identity providers and service providers support the same SCIM version prevents schema mismatches and unexpected API behavior. Service providers should publish SCIM compliance documentation detailing supported attributes, request formats, and authentication mechanisms.

Monitoring and logging SCIM activity provide valuable insights into troubleshooting recurring issues. Centralized logging solutions such as Splunk, ELK Stack, or Azure Monitor can aggregate SCIM logs and generate alerts based on error patterns. Metrics such as request latency, success rates, and error rates should be monitored to detect performance degradation and unexpected failures. Establishing proactive monitoring allows administrators to address SCIM issues before they impact identity synchronization.

Automated testing ensures that SCIM implementations remain reliable across updates and configuration changes. Running test cases for user provisioning, attribute updates, and deprovisioning operations helps validate SCIM integrations. Simulating high API request loads in test environments can identify potential scalability issues before deploying SCIM solutions in production. Continuous integration and continuous deployment (CI/CD) pipelines should include SCIM testing to prevent regressions in identity synchronization workflows.

SCIM troubleshooting requires a systematic approach that involves analyzing authentication errors, debugging API requests, optimizing performance, and monitoring system behavior. Ensuring that SCIM configurations align across identity providers and service providers reduces synchronization failures. By implementing structured logging, proactive monitoring, and automated testing, organizations can maintain a stable and efficient SCIM deployment that supports scalable identity management.

SCIM Logs and Monitoring

SCIM logs and monitoring are essential for maintaining a reliable, secure, and scalable identity management system. Logs provide visibility into identity synchronization activities, while monitoring ensures real-time detection of issues affecting SCIM performance, security, and compliance. Organizations using SCIM must implement robust logging and monitoring strategies to track provisioning events, troubleshoot synchronization failures, detect unauthorized access attempts, and optimize system performance.

SCIM logs capture detailed records of API requests and responses, providing a chronological history of identity management operations. Each SCIM request generates a log entry containing relevant metadata, including the request method, endpoint, status code, timestamps, and request payload. Log entries for user provisioning, updates, deletions, and authentication events help administrators analyze system behavior and identify issues. By maintaining structured SCIM logs, organizations gain insight into how identity data is processed and propagated across integrated applications.

Authentication and authorization logs play a critical role in SCIM security. SCIM relies on OAuth 2.0 for API authentication, and logs must capture token validation attempts, failed login attempts, and token expiration events. If a SCIM client fails to authenticate, logs should indicate whether the issue is due to an expired token, incorrect credentials, or insufficient permissions. Authorization logs record whether API requests comply with assigned scopes, ensuring that SCIM clients only perform actions within their permitted access levels.

Provisioning logs track user account creation across connected applications. When a new user is provisioned, logs should record the identity attributes included in the request, the service provider receiving the request, and the success or failure of the operation. If a provisioning request fails, logs should provide detailed error messages explaining missing attributes, schema mismatches, or permission-related issues. Reviewing provisioning logs enables administrators to identify and resolve misconfigurations affecting user account synchronization.

Update logs document changes to user attributes, such as email updates, role modifications, and department changes. Each update request should generate a log entry specifying the modified attributes, the identity provider initiating the change, and the status of the request. If updates fail, logs should capture validation errors or conflicting attribute mappings. Ensuring that SCIM logs retain historical update records allows organizations to track identity modifications over time and detect inconsistencies.

Deprovisioning logs record user account removals and access revocations. When a user is deactivated or deleted, SCIM logs should confirm whether the deprovisioning request was successfully processed across all applications. If a deprovisioning request fails, logs should indicate whether the target account was already removed, whether the service provider supports DELETE operations, or whether alternative methods such as setting active=false were used. Proper deprovisioning logs help organizations verify that inactive accounts are promptly revoked, reducing security risks associated with orphaned accounts.

Error logs capture SCIM API failures, network issues, and unexpected behavior. Common SCIM errors include 400 Bad Request for invalid payloads, 401 Unauthorized for authentication failures, 403 Forbidden for insufficient permissions, and 500 Internal Server Error for server-side failures. Detailed error messages help administrators diagnose and resolve issues affecting SCIM synchronization. Error logs should be monitored continuously to detect patterns indicating systemic problems, such as repeated authentication failures or misconfigured identity attributes.

Performance logs track SCIM API response times, request volumes, and server load. High API latency may indicate network congestion, database bottlenecks, or inefficient API queries. By monitoring performance logs, organizations can optimize SCIM implementations by implementing pagination, caching, and load balancing. Performance metrics such as request throughput, error rates, and processing time should be analyzed to ensure SCIM operates efficiently under varying workloads.

SCIM monitoring involves real-time tracking of identity synchronization activities, security events, and system performance. Monitoring solutions aggregate SCIM logs and generate alerts based on predefined thresholds. If SCIM API request failures exceed acceptable levels or response times become too high, monitoring tools trigger alerts to notify administrators. Organizations use monitoring dashboards to visualize SCIM metrics, identify trends, and take proactive measures to prevent service disruptions.

Security monitoring detects unauthorized SCIM activity, such as brute-force authentication attempts, API key misuse, or privilege escalation. Identity-related anomalies, such as sudden bulk provisioning of accounts or unexpected role changes, should generate alerts for further investigation. Integrating SCIM logs with Security Information and Event Management (SIEM) solutions enhances threat detection by correlating SCIM events with broader security insights.

Audit logs provide a compliance trail for identity-related activities. Regulations such as GDPR, CCPA, and HIPAA require organizations to maintain records of identity access and modifications. SCIM audit logs track identity creation, attribute updates, and deprovisioning actions to demonstrate compliance with data protection policies. Administrators should regularly review audit logs to verify that SCIM operations align with corporate security and regulatory requirements.

SCIM log retention policies determine how long identity synchronization records are stored. Organizations should define retention periods based on compliance requirements, security policies, and operational needs. Short-term logs facilitate real-time debugging, while long-term logs support forensic investigations and compliance audits. Secure storage and encryption of SCIM logs prevent unauthorized access and tampering.

Centralized logging solutions improve SCIM log management by consolidating log data across multiple SCIM endpoints and identity providers. Organizations use platforms such as Splunk, ELK Stack, Azure Monitor, or AWS CloudWatch to aggregate SCIM logs and enable advanced search and analysis capabilities. Centralized logging simplifies troubleshooting by providing a unified view of SCIM activity across the entire identity management ecosystem.

Log correlation links SCIM events with other security and operational logs to provide a holistic view of identity management. Correlating SCIM logs with authentication logs, application access logs, and network activity logs helps organizations detect security threats and operational issues. If a SCIM provisioning request corresponds with suspicious login attempts, correlating logs can reveal potential identity compromise incidents.

Automated log analysis enhances SCIM monitoring by using machine learning and anomaly detection to identify unusual patterns in SCIM activity. AI-driven security analytics can detect deviations from normal provisioning behavior, flagging potential insider threats or compromised accounts. Automated alerts ensure that security teams receive immediate notifications of suspicious SCIM events, enabling rapid response.

SCIM monitoring dashboards provide real-time visualization of key metrics, including synchronization success rates, API latency, and user provisioning trends. Customizable dashboards allow administrators to monitor SCIM health, identify performance bottlenecks, and ensure seamless identity synchronization. By analyzing SCIM monitoring data, organizations can optimize API performance, improve security posture, and enhance overall identity management efficiency.

Testing and validating SCIM logging configurations ensure that logs capture all necessary identity events. Organizations should conduct periodic log audits to verify completeness and accuracy. Testing tools such as Postman or API monitoring platforms can be used to simulate SCIM requests and validate log entries. Continuous monitoring of log integrity ensures that SCIM logs remain a reliable source of identity data.

SCIM logging and monitoring are critical for maintaining secure, efficient, and compliant identity synchronization. Implementing structured log management, real-time monitoring, and security analytics enables organizations to detect issues early, optimize SCIM performance, and safeguard identity data. By leveraging centralized logging solutions and proactive monitoring strategies, organizations ensure that SCIM remains a robust and scalable identity management framework.

SCIM API Versioning Strategies

SCIM (System for Cross-domain Identity Management) is a standardized protocol designed to facilitate the exchange of identity information across different systems. As with any API, SCIM evolves over time, requiring a well-defined versioning strategy to ensure compatibility, stability, and seamless integration for clients and service providers. Versioning strategies are crucial to managing changes, minimizing disruptions, and maintaining backward compatibility when introducing new features, deprecating old ones, or fixing issues.

One of the most common versioning approaches in SCIM APIs is URL-based versioning. This method involves embedding the version number directly in the API's URL, such as /v1/Users or /v2/Groups. By doing so, different API versions can coexist, allowing clients to migrate at their own pace. This strategy ensures that existing integrations remain functional while providing a clear path for upgrades. However, it also requires maintaining multiple versions simultaneously, which can increase operational overhead.

Another widely used versioning strategy is header-based versioning. In this approach, the API version is specified in the request headers rather than the URL. For example, a client might include a custom header such as X-SCIM-Version: 2.0. This method helps keep URLs clean and can offer more flexibility, as different clients can request different versions without modifying their endpoints. However, this approach may require additional effort in documentation and client configuration, as the version is not as easily identifiable as when it is embedded in the URL.

Schema versioning is another important consideration in SCIM. Since SCIM relies on JSON-based schemas to define user and group attributes, schema changes must be managed carefully. Adding new attributes is generally a backward-compatible change, but modifying or removing existing attributes can break client implementations. To handle schema evolution, SCIM APIs often include metadata that specifies schema versions, allowing clients to determine whether they support a particular version of an object. Providing detailed documentation on schema changes and offering transitional periods before deprecating old attributes can help mitigate issues.

Deprecation policies play a key role in SCIM API versioning strategies. When a new version is introduced, service providers must decide how long they will support older versions and how they will notify clients about upcoming changes. A well-defined deprecation strategy typically includes advance notices, clear timelines, and versioning roadmaps. Providing deprecation warnings in API responses, such as including a Deprecated header with a recommended migration path, can help clients plan for updates. Additionally, maintaining changelogs and release notes allows developers to track modifications and assess their impact.

Backward compatibility is a fundamental principle in SCIM API versioning. Many organizations strive to ensure that newer versions do not break existing integrations. One way to achieve this is by following additive changes, meaning new features and attributes are introduced without altering existing functionality. However, when breaking changes are unavoidable, offering migration guides, running parallel versions, and providing sandbox environments for testing can ease the transition for clients. Testing tools and validation mechanisms can further assist developers in ensuring compatibility with new versions.

Feature toggles and version negotiation mechanisms can enhance flexibility in SCIM API versioning. Instead of relying solely on static version numbers, some APIs allow clients to request specific features through query parameters or headers. For instance, a client could specify ?features=extendedSchemas to enable a new capability without upgrading to a major version. This approach allows gradual adoption of new functionalities while reducing the need for strict version increments.

Security considerations also influence SCIM API versioning decisions. As security vulnerabilities are discovered, patches and security enhancements may need to be applied across multiple API versions. Ensuring that older versions receive critical security updates while encouraging clients to move to more secure versions is a delicate balance. Communicating security-related changes transparently and enforcing security best practices, such as requiring OAuth 2.0 for authentication, can help maintain a robust and secure SCIM implementation.

Performance and scalability are additional factors in versioning strategies. As SCIM APIs evolve, they may introduce optimizations that improve efficiency. However, older versions might still rely on legacy implementations that are less efficient. To manage this, service providers need to monitor API usage, gradually phase out outdated versions, and encourage clients to adopt newer, more performant alternatives. Rate limiting, caching strategies, and query optimizations can also play a role in managing API performance across multiple versions.

Testing and validation frameworks are essential components of a successful SCIM API versioning strategy. Automated tests should cover multiple API versions to ensure that new releases do not introduce regressions. Providing sample requests and responses for each version, along with SDKs and client libraries, can further simplify integration for developers. Additionally, offering API validation tools that allow clients to test their implementations against different versions can help detect compatibility issues early.

Adopting a comprehensive documentation strategy is vital for effective SCIM API versioning. Clear and detailed API documentation should outline versioning policies, supported versions, deprecation schedules, and migration guides. Interactive API explorers and sandbox environments can further aid developers in understanding and testing different API versions. Keeping documentation up to date and accessible ensures that clients can make informed decisions about their integrations.

Industry best practices for SCIM API versioning continue to evolve as organizations gain experience with identity management at scale. Learning from real-world implementations, gathering feedback from developers, and iterating on versioning strategies are all crucial for maintaining a stable and user-friendly API. By balancing innovation with stability, organizations can ensure that their SCIM APIs remain reliable, secure, and adaptable to future identity management challenges.

SCIM Custom Attributes and Extensions

SCIM (System for Cross-domain Identity Management) is a standardized protocol designed to streamline the management of identity information across different systems. While SCIM provides a well-defined core schema that covers common user and group attributes, many organizations require additional attributes to meet their unique business needs. To accommodate these requirements, SCIM allows for the use of custom attributes and schema extensions, enabling greater flexibility while maintaining interoperability with the standard framework.

Custom attributes play a critical role in extending the functionality of SCIM without disrupting its standardized nature. Organizations often need to store additional identity-related data that is not included in the default SCIM schema. These attributes can range from job-related information, such as department codes and security clearance levels, to application-specific details that are required for integration with internal systems. By defining custom attributes, organizations can ensure that SCIM serves as a centralized and comprehensive identity management solution without requiring external modifications or workarounds.

To implement custom attributes, service providers typically extend the SCIM schema by adding new attribute definitions. This extension mechanism allows for the inclusion of additional fields within the user or group resources while preserving compliance with the SCIM specification. Custom attributes must be properly defined within the schema to ensure compatibility with client applications. This involves specifying attribute properties such as name, data type, mutability, and whether the attribute is required. Properly defining these attributes ensures that they are consistently interpreted across different SCIM implementations.

Schema extensions in SCIM offer a more structured way to incorporate custom attributes while maintaining a clear distinction between standard and non-standard fields. Extensions allow organizations to group related custom attributes into separate namespaces, reducing conflicts and improving manageability. For example, an organization might define an extension specifically for employee-related attributes, such as work location, contract type, or supervisor information. This approach ensures that additional attributes do not interfere with the core SCIM schema while enabling clients to access only the data they need.

One of the key benefits of using schema extensions is that they allow for modular customization without altering the core SCIM resources. Extensions are typically referenced in API responses by including an extension-specific namespace, which enables clients to differentiate between standard attributes and custom attributes. This separation enhances interoperability by allowing SCIM implementations to support extensions without requiring changes to their fundamental structure. When a SCIM client interacts with an API that includes extensions, it can choose to process only the core attributes or leverage the extended attributes if needed.

Managing custom attributes and extensions effectively requires careful consideration of schema evolution and backward compatibility. As organizations refine their identity management processes, they may need to introduce new attributes, modify existing ones, or deprecate outdated attributes. Adding new attributes is generally non-disruptive, as SCIM clients can ignore unknown attributes without affecting their functionality. However, modifying or removing attributes can introduce compatibility challenges, especially if client applications rely on specific fields. To address this, organizations should establish versioning strategies and provide clear documentation on schema changes.

Security considerations are also important when implementing custom attributes and extensions in SCIM. Since SCIM is often used to manage sensitive identity data, custom attributes should adhere to security best practices, including proper access controls and encryption mechanisms. Some attributes, such as personally identifiable information (PII) or access control policies, may require additional safeguards to prevent unauthorized access. Service providers should implement role-based access control (RBAC) and other authorization mechanisms to ensure that only authorized clients can retrieve or modify specific attributes.

Performance optimization is another key aspect of working with SCIM custom attributes and extensions. Since SCIM is designed for high-volume identity operations, service providers must ensure that custom attributes do not negatively impact API performance. Large attribute sets or complex data structures can increase response payload sizes, leading to higher latency and bandwidth usage. Implementing selective attribute retrieval through query parameters or filtering mechanisms can help optimize performance by allowing clients to request only the attributes they need. Additionally, caching strategies and database indexing can improve query efficiency when dealing with extended schemas.

Standardization and interoperability remain critical challenges when implementing custom attributes and extensions. While SCIM provides a flexible framework for customization, different organizations may define similar attributes in different ways, leading to inconsistencies across implementations. To mitigate this issue, industry-wide best practices and common extension schemas have emerged, allowing organizations to adopt predefined attribute sets for specific use cases. Following established extension standards can improve compatibility and reduce the need for custom implementations when integrating with third-party SCIM providers.

Proper documentation and communication are essential for the successful adoption of SCIM custom attributes and extensions. Organizations should maintain up-to-date schema documentation that outlines all custom attributes, their definitions, and their intended use cases. Providing example API requests and responses that include extended attributes can help developers understand how to interact with the customized SCIM API. Additionally, organizations should communicate schema changes effectively to ensure that client applications remain compatible with new versions of the SCIM implementation.

Testing and validation play a crucial role in ensuring that SCIM custom attributes and extensions function as expected. Automated tests should verify that custom attributes are correctly processed by both the SCIM provider and client applications. Validation tools can help detect schema inconsistencies, enforce attribute constraints, and ensure compliance with SCIM specifications. Conducting thorough testing before deploying schema changes can prevent integration issues and minimize disruptions for end users.

As SCIM adoption continues to grow, the ability to define and manage custom attributes and extensions will remain a key factor in its success. Organizations that leverage SCIM for identity management must strike a balance between flexibility and standardization to ensure a seamless integration experience. By following best practices for defining, securing, and optimizing custom attributes, organizations can extend SCIM in a way that meets their unique business needs while maintaining compatibility with the broader identity management ecosystem.

SCIM and Identity Governance

SCIM (System for Cross-domain Identity Management) plays a crucial role in modern identity governance by providing a standardized approach to managing user identities across different systems. Identity governance involves enforcing policies, ensuring compliance, and managing user access in a secure and controlled manner. SCIM enhances these processes by automating identity provisioning, deprovisioning, and synchronization while maintaining consistency across multiple applications and platforms. By integrating SCIM with identity governance solutions, organizations can strengthen security, improve efficiency, and reduce the risks associated with manual identity management.

One of the key aspects of identity governance is access control, which ensures that users have the right level of access to resources based on their roles and responsibilities. SCIM helps enforce access control policies by streamlining the assignment of roles and permissions through automated user provisioning. When a new employee joins an organization, SCIM can facilitate the automatic creation of their user account, assign them to the appropriate groups, and grant access to required applications based on predefined policies. This reduces the administrative burden on IT teams and minimizes the risk of human error in access assignments.

Identity lifecycle management is another critical component of identity governance that benefits from SCIM. Throughout an employee's tenure, their role and responsibilities may change, requiring adjustments to their access privileges. SCIM enables real-time updates to user attributes and group memberships, ensuring that changes are reflected across all connected systems. When an employee is promoted, SCIM can automatically update their access rights to match their new role, ensuring that they have the necessary permissions while removing access that is no longer needed. This dynamic approach helps organizations maintain compliance with security policies and reduces the risk of unauthorized access.

The deprovisioning of users is an essential aspect of identity governance that SCIM simplifies. When an employee leaves the organization, it is critical to revoke their access to prevent potential security breaches. Without automated deprovisioning, former employees may retain access to sensitive systems, increasing the risk of data leaks and insider threats. SCIM facilitates deprovisioning by ensuring that user accounts are automatically disabled or removed across all integrated applications when a termination event is detected. This reduces the likelihood of orphaned accounts and helps organizations enforce strict offboarding policies.

Compliance and auditability are fundamental to identity governance, as organizations must demonstrate adherence to regulatory requirements and internal policies. SCIM contributes to compliance efforts by maintaining a consistent and auditable record of identity changes across all systems. Every user creation, modification, and deletion is recorded, providing organizations with a comprehensive audit trail. This level of transparency is essential for meeting regulatory requirements such as GDPR, HIPAA, and SOX, which mandate strict controls over identity and access management. By leveraging SCIM's standardized approach to identity management, organizations can generate detailed reports on user access and ensure that compliance audits are conducted efficiently.

Another key benefit of SCIM in identity governance is its ability to integrate with identity governance and administration (IGA) platforms. These platforms provide centralized control over user identities, access certifications, and policy enforcement. SCIM enables seamless synchronization between IGA solutions and downstream applications, ensuring that governance policies are consistently applied across all connected systems. Organizations can define role-based access controls, enforce separation-of-duties policies, and conduct periodic access reviews with greater accuracy by leveraging SCIM's automated data exchange capabilities.

Risk management is an important aspect of identity governance, as organizations must proactively identify and mitigate security threats. SCIM enhances risk management by ensuring that identity data remains accurate and up to date across all systems. When identity information is inconsistent or outdated, it can create security gaps that attackers can exploit. SCIM reduces these risks by ensuring that user attributes and access rights are continuously synchronized, eliminating discrepancies that could lead to unauthorized access. Additionally, SCIM supports integration with security information and event management (SIEM) systems, enabling real-time monitoring and alerting on suspicious identity-related activities.

The scalability of SCIM makes it well-suited for large enterprises and cloud-based environments where identity governance requirements are complex. As organizations grow and adopt more cloud applications, managing user identities manually becomes increasingly challenging. SCIM provides a scalable solution by allowing identity governance processes to be automated across thousands of users and applications. This scalability ensures that identity governance remains effective even as the organization expands, reducing administrative overhead while maintaining security and compliance.

Identity governance also involves managing privileged access, ensuring that high-risk accounts receive special scrutiny. SCIM can be used in conjunction with privileged access management (PAM) solutions to control access to critical systems. By automating the provisioning and deprovisioning of privileged accounts, SCIM helps organizations enforce the principle of least privilege, ensuring that users only have access to the resources necessary for their roles. This minimizes the risk of privilege abuse and enhances security by reducing the attack surface.

Effective identity governance requires strong policy enforcement, and SCIM contributes to this by ensuring that access policies are consistently applied across all systems. Organizations can define policies that dictate who can access specific applications, how long access is granted, and under what conditions access should be revoked. SCIM automates the enforcement of these policies by synchronizing identity data across all integrated platforms. This level of consistency helps prevent security gaps and ensures that access management aligns with organizational policies.

The adoption of SCIM in identity governance continues to grow as organizations recognize the benefits of a standardized approach to identity management. By automating user provisioning, enforcing access control policies, and improving auditability, SCIM enhances security and compliance efforts while reducing administrative overhead. As identity governance evolves, SCIM will remain a critical component in helping organizations manage identities efficiently and securely in an increasingly complex digital landscape.

Migrating to SCIM from Legacy Systems

Migrating from legacy identity management systems to SCIM (System for Cross-domain Identity Management) presents organizations with an opportunity to modernize their identity lifecycle management processes while improving efficiency, security, and interoperability. Legacy systems often rely on custom-built provisioning mechanisms, proprietary connectors, or manual workflows that are difficult to scale and maintain. SCIM offers a standardized and automated approach to identity management, enabling seamless integration across cloud and on-premises applications. Transitioning to SCIM requires careful planning, data transformation, and process alignment to ensure a smooth migration with minimal disruption to existing operations.

One of the first steps in migrating to SCIM is assessing the current identity infrastructure and understanding how user provisioning and deprovisioning are managed within the legacy system. Many organizations use LDAP-based directories, custom scripts, or API-driven connectors that handle identity synchronization. These solutions often operate in a fragmented manner, leading to inconsistencies and security risks due to outdated or orphaned accounts. A thorough audit of existing identity sources, attributes, and synchronization rules helps identify gaps, redundant processes, and opportunities for optimization. Organizations should document how user identities are created, updated, and removed across all connected systems before designing their SCIM implementation.

Data transformation is a critical aspect of the migration process, as SCIM operates on a well-defined schema that may differ from the attribute structures used in legacy systems. User attributes such as names, email addresses, job titles, and department codes must be mapped to their corresponding SCIM attributes. In some cases, legacy systems contain non-standard or application-specific attributes that need to be handled through SCIM extensions. Data cleansing is an important step to remove duplicates, standardize formatting, and ensure that only relevant identity records are migrated. Organizations should also consider defining attribute validation rules to enforce consistency in the SCIM implementation.

Interoperability with existing applications is another key consideration during migration. Many enterprise applications rely on identity provisioning mechanisms that were designed before SCIM became widely adopted. Some applications may still require direct database updates, proprietary APIs, or batch-based synchronization. Organizations must evaluate which applications can natively support SCIM, which require additional configuration, and which need intermediary solutions such as middleware or API gateways. For applications that do not support SCIM directly, custom connectors or transformation layers can be developed to translate SCIM-based identity updates into the required format.

Security and access control policies must be aligned with SCIM's capabilities to ensure a secure migration. Legacy systems often have different authorization models and permission structures that need to be mapped to SCIM-based role and group management. Organizations should review how access is granted, inherited, and revoked within the legacy system and determine how these policies will be enforced in the new SCIM-enabled architecture. Implementing role-based access control (RBAC) and least-privilege principles helps maintain a secure environment while streamlining access provisioning across applications.

Testing and validation are essential to ensuring a successful SCIM migration. Before fully transitioning, organizations should conduct pilot implementations with a subset of users to evaluate data integrity, synchronization accuracy, and system compatibility. Testing should include creating, updating, and deleting user records to confirm that identity changes are correctly propagated across all integrated systems. Organizations should also perform security testing to verify that unauthorized access is prevented and that SCIM endpoints are properly protected with authentication mechanisms such as OAuth 2.0. By identifying and addressing potential issues early, organizations can reduce the risk of service disruptions when migrating at scale.

Phased migration strategies help mitigate risks and allow organizations to transition incrementally. Instead of attempting a complete cutover to SCIM in a single deployment, a phased approach enables gradual adoption while maintaining legacy processes as a fallback. One approach is to start with non-critical user groups or specific applications before expanding to the entire organization. Running SCIM alongside the legacy system in a hybrid mode can also provide a safety net, allowing administrators to validate identity synchronization before fully decommissioning the old infrastructure. Monitoring and logging identity events during this transition help track discrepancies and fine-tune the SCIM implementation.

User communication and change management play a vital role in the migration process, as employees, IT teams, and application owners need to understand how the new identity management approach will impact them. Organizations should provide clear documentation, training sessions, and support resources to ensure a smooth transition. End users may need guidance on updated authentication processes, role assignments, or self-service capabilities introduced by SCIM. IT administrators should be equipped with troubleshooting guidelines and monitoring tools to handle potential issues during and after migration. Establishing a feedback loop with stakeholders allows for continuous improvements and ensures that the SCIM deployment meets organizational needs.

Long-term maintenance and optimization of the SCIM implementation require ongoing monitoring and adaptation. As business requirements evolve, new applications may need to be integrated, and existing identity policies may require updates. Organizations should establish governance practices to regularly review SCIM configurations, security policies, and performance metrics. Automating compliance checks and access reviews can help maintain data integrity and regulatory adherence. Additionally, keeping up with SCIM standard updates and industry best practices ensures that the implementation remains aligned with modern identity management trends.

Migrating to SCIM from legacy systems represents a significant step toward modernizing identity management, improving automation, and enhancing security. By carefully planning the transition, aligning data structures, and implementing robust testing strategies, organizations can achieve a seamless migration with minimal disruption. Leveraging SCIM's standardized approach enables greater interoperability, scalability, and efficiency, ultimately providing a future-proof identity management solution that meets the evolving needs of businesses and enterprises.

Case Studies: SCIM in Real-World Implementations

SCIM (System for Cross domain Identity Management) has become a critical component in modern identity management strategies, helping organizations streamline user provisioning, automate access control, and maintain compliance with security standards. Real-world implementations of SCIM showcase its ability to simplify identity synchronization across multiple applications while reducing administrative overhead. Organizations from different industries, including technology, finance, healthcare, and education, have successfully leveraged SCIM to solve complex identity management challenges. Examining case studies of SCIM implementations provides insights into the benefits, challenges, and best practices associated with deploying the standard in various environments.

A global technology company with thousands of employees and contractors faced significant challenges in managing user accounts across a wide range of internal and cloud-based applications. Their existing identity management system relied on manual provisioning and deprovisioning processes, leading to delays in granting access and increased security risks due to orphaned accounts. By implementing SCIM, the company automated the user lifecycle process, ensuring that new hires received appropriate access on their first day and that departing employees were deprovisioned immediately upon termination. The SCIM-based solution integrated with the company's HR system, triggering automatic updates whenever employee status or department assignments changed. This not only improved security by eliminating stale accounts but also enhanced efficiency by reducing IT workload and eliminating manual errors.

A financial services firm needed to ensure strict compliance with regulatory requirements while managing user identities across a mix of legacy and cloud-based applications. The firm's previous identity management system relied on custom-built scripts and periodic batch synchronizations, which often resulted in outdated user records and access discrepancies. By transitioning to a SCIM-based identity provisioning model, the firm achieved real-time synchronization of user attributes across its authentication platforms, reducing the risk of unauthorized access. The SCIM integration also enabled automated access reviews, ensuring that access rights were regularly audited and aligned with the firm's security policies. By adopting SCIM, the firm improved its compliance posture and reduced the risk of financial penalties associated with security breaches and audit failures.

A large healthcare provider operating multiple hospitals and clinics faced difficulties managing identities across electronic health record (EHR) systems, clinical applications, and third-party services. The complexity of managing access to sensitive patient data made security and compliance a top priority. Before implementing SCIM, the healthcare provider struggled with inconsistencies in user roles and permissions, often leading to delays in access provisioning for new medical staff. By deploying a SCIM-enabled identity platform, the organization established centralized control over user access, ensuring that medical professionals could access necessary systems without unnecessary delays. The SCIM integration also allowed for real-time role adjustments based on staff reassignments, ensuring that access was granted only when necessary. This implementation significantly improved operational efficiency while maintaining compliance with healthcare regulations such as HIPAA.

A multinational retail corporation required a scalable identity management solution to support its growing workforce, which included full-time employees, seasonal workers, and external vendors. The company's previous identity management approach relied on a combination of manual account creation and proprietary connectors, resulting in inconsistencies across applications. By adopting SCIM, the company standardized user provisioning across its entire ecosystem, ensuring that employees and contractors had seamless access to necessary applications based on their roles. The SCIM implementation integrated with the company's workforce management system, allowing for automatic provisioning and deprovisioning of temporary workers based on predefined employment periods. This improved security by ensuring that short-term employees did not retain access beyond their contractual terms while simplifying onboarding and offboarding processes.

An educational institution with a diverse user base of students, faculty, and administrative staff sought a more efficient way to manage identity provisioning across its learning management system (LMS), research platforms, and administrative applications. Before implementing SCIM, IT administrators had to manually create and deactivate accounts, leading to delays in student and faculty access. With the adoption of SCIM, the institution automated user account creation based on enrollment records, ensuring that students had immediate access to coursework and digital resources upon registration. Faculty accounts were automatically updated based on employment status, ensuring that professors and researchers had access only while actively employed. The SCIM implementation also facilitated collaboration between different departments by enabling seamless access to shared academic tools. By streamlining identity management, the institution enhanced the overall student and faculty experience while reducing the administrative burden on IT teams.

A cloud-based software company offering SaaS solutions to enterprises faced increasing demand for automated identity provisioning from its customers. Many of the company's clients required integration with their existing identity providers to streamline user access. To meet this need, the company implemented SCIM support in its application, enabling customers to automatically synchronize users and groups from their corporate directories. This eliminated the need for manual user account management, allowing customers to scale their deployments more efficiently. The SCIM integration also improved security by ensuring that user accounts in the SaaS platform were always in sync with the customer's identity provider. By adopting SCIM, the software company enhanced its product's appeal to enterprise customers while reducing support requests related to identity synchronization issues.

A government agency managing access to sensitive data across multiple departments sought a secure and standardized approach to identity management. The agency faced challenges in maintaining a centralized identity repository while allowing for decentralized access control within individual departments. By deploying SCIM, the agency established a federated identity management system that allowed for real-time identity updates across different government applications. SCIM's extensibility enabled the agency to define custom attributes specific to government operations while maintaining compliance with national security regulations. The implementation improved identity governance by ensuring that access rights were strictly enforced based on an individual's role and security clearance level. This enhanced security while reducing administrative overhead associated with managing user accounts across multiple agencies.

Real-world implementations of SCIM highlight its ability to address identity management challenges across different industries and organizational structures. Whether streamlining user provisioning, enhancing security, ensuring compliance, or improving operational efficiency, SCIM provides a standardized and scalable solution that simplifies identity synchronization. Organizations that adopt SCIM benefit from reduced administrative burden, improved access control, and seamless integration with both legacy and cloud-based applications. By learning from successful SCIM deployments, enterprises can develop best practices for implementing the standard in their own environments, ensuring a secure and efficient approach to identity management.

SCIM Best Practices and Pitfalls

SCIM (System for Cross-domain Identity Management) provides a standardized framework for managing user identities across multiple applications and services. By automating identity provisioning, synchronization, and deprovisioning, SCIM enhances security and efficiency while reducing administrative overhead. However, implementing SCIM requires careful planning, adherence to best practices, and awareness of common pitfalls that can impact performance, security, and maintainability. Organizations that adopt SCIM must focus on designing scalable and secure implementations while avoiding mistakes that could lead to data inconsistencies, integration failures, or security vulnerabilities.

One of the best practices in SCIM implementation is ensuring schema consistency and proper attribute mapping. SCIM defines a core schema for user and group attributes, but organizations often need to extend this schema to accommodate custom attributes specific to their business needs. Properly defining these attributes and maintaining a clear mapping between SCIM attributes and internal identity stores is essential for seamless synchronization. Organizations should document attribute transformations, enforce validation rules, and avoid unnecessary attribute proliferation, which can lead to complexity and maintenance challenges. Ensuring that attributes follow standardized naming conventions improves interoperability and reduces integration errors.

Another key best practice is designing for scalability and performance. SCIM is often used in environments where thousands or even millions of users must be synchronized across applications. To handle large-scale identity operations efficiently, organizations should implement pagination and filtering mechanisms when querying SCIM endpoints. Instead of retrieving all users in a single request, clients should use SCIM's pagination support to fetch data in manageable chunks.

Similarly, implementing delta queries—where only changed or new records are retrieved—can significantly reduce the load on the SCIM service. Optimizing database indexing and caching strategies also helps improve response times and reduces strain on identity management systems.

Authentication and security play a critical role in SCIM deployments. Since SCIM involves handling sensitive identity information, strong authentication mechanisms such as OAuth 2.0 should be enforced for API access. Organizations should avoid hardcoding credentials in configuration files and instead use secure authentication tokens that follow industry best practices. Implementing role-based access control (RBAC) ensures that only authorized applications and users can interact with SCIM endpoints. Additionally, enforcing rate limiting and request throttling helps prevent abuse and protects SCIM services from denial-of-service attacks. Logging and monitoring API requests allow organizations to detect and respond to suspicious activities in real time.

Effective error handling and logging are crucial for maintaining a robust SCIM implementation. API interactions can fail due to various reasons, such as network issues, schema mismatches, or unauthorized access attempts. Properly structured error responses using standard SCIM error codes help clients understand and address issues efficiently. Logging SCIM API requests and responses with sufficient detail enables troubleshooting and auditability. However, organizations must ensure that sensitive user data is not logged in plaintext to prevent security risks. Implementing structured logging and integrating with centralized log management solutions enhances visibility into SCIM operations.

One of the common pitfalls in SCIM implementation is failing to handle user lifecycle events properly. SCIM enables automated provisioning, updates, and deprovisioning, but misconfigurations in lifecycle policies can lead to unintended consequences. For example, improper handling of user terminations can result in orphaned accounts remaining active, increasing security risks. On the other hand, overly aggressive deprovisioning policies may remove access prematurely, disrupting business operations. Organizations should establish clear lifecycle policies that define when users should be created, updated, or removed from applications. Implementing soft-delete mechanisms where user accounts are deactivated before permanent deletion can provide a safeguard against accidental data loss.

Another pitfall is neglecting backward compatibility when updating SCIM implementations. As organizations refine their SCIM deployments, schema modifications and API changes may be required. However, introducing breaking changes without considering existing integrations can cause disruptions for clients consuming SCIM services. To prevent this, organizations should adopt versioning strategies that allow clients to continue using older versions while gradually migrating to newer ones. Providing clear deprecation notices, transition periods, and migration guides helps ensure a smooth upgrade path. Testing SCIM changes in a sandbox environment before deploying them to production minimizes the risk of unintended consequences.

Failing to properly test SCIM integrations is another common mistake that can lead to synchronization failures and data inconsistencies. SCIM implementations should undergo comprehensive testing, including functional testing, performance testing, and security testing. Organizations should simulate real-world scenarios, such as bulk user provisioning, role changes, and deprovisioning workflows, to ensure that identity data remains consistent across systems. Automated testing frameworks can help validate SCIM endpoints against expected behaviors, reducing the likelihood of errors in production. Establishing test environments that mirror production settings allows teams to validate SCIM changes without impacting live users.

Maintaining comprehensive documentation is essential for successful SCIM adoption. Organizations often overlook the importance of clear and up-to-date documentation, leading to confusion among developers and administrators. SCIM documentation should cover API endpoints, authentication mechanisms, attribute mappings, expected request and response formats, and error handling guidelines. Providing sample API requests and responses helps developers understand how to interact with the SCIM service effectively. Keeping documentation aligned with SCIM schema updates and API changes ensures that clients and internal teams can integrate with the service smoothly.

Ensuring interoperability with different SCIM clients and identity providers is another best practice. SCIM is designed to facilitate cross-platform identity synchronization, but variations in implementations can lead to compatibility issues. Organizations should test their SCIM endpoints with multiple identity providers and applications to verify compliance with the SCIM specification. Adhering to the SCIM standard as closely as possible helps prevent integration challenges and promotes seamless interoperability. Where necessary, organizations should provide configuration guides and support for third-party applications to simplify integration efforts.

SCIM implementation success depends on aligning identity governance policies with technical configurations. Organizations must define clear governance policies that specify how user identities should be managed across systems, including access control rules, deprovisioning timelines, and audit requirements. Aligning SCIM configurations with identity governance policies ensures that identity data remains secure, compliant, and up to date. Regular reviews of identity synchronization policies help organizations adapt to evolving security and compliance requirements.

By following best practices and avoiding common pitfalls, organizations can leverage SCIM to create an efficient, secure, and scalable identity management framework. Proper schema design, authentication security, lifecycle management, error handling, interoperability testing, and documentation all contribute to a successful SCIM implementation. Organizations that approach SCIM deployment strategically can achieve seamless identity synchronization while minimizing risks and operational complexities.

SCIM and the Future of Identity Management

SCIM (System for Cross-domain Identity Management) has established itself as a fundamental standard for managing user identities across multiple systems, applications, and platforms. As organizations continue to expand their digital ecosystems, the need for seamless identity synchronization and automated provisioning has become more critical than ever. The future of identity management is being shaped by trends such as decentralized identity, zero trust security, artificial intelligence, and the growing adoption of cloud-based services. SCIM will play a crucial role in these developments by evolving to meet new security, scalability, and interoperability demands while integrating with emerging identity technologies.

One of the key trends influencing the future of identity management is the shift toward decentralized identity. Traditional identity management models rely on centralized directories and federated authentication mechanisms to verify user credentials. However, decentralized identity frameworks, such as those based on blockchain and self-sovereign identity (SSI), aim to give users greater control over their digital identities. In this model, users manage their own identity attributes and share them selectively with organizations rather than relying on a single identity provider. SCIM can be adapted to support decentralized identity architectures by facilitating the synchronization of verified identity claims across trusted systems. As decentralized identity gains traction, SCIM implementations will need to incorporate mechanisms for handling distributed identity attributes while maintaining security and compliance.

Zero trust security is another major factor shaping the evolution of identity management. The traditional perimeter-based security model, which assumes that users and devices within a corporate network are inherently trusted, is becoming obsolete. Zero trust security principles require continuous verification of user identities, device trustworthiness, and access conditions before granting access to resources. SCIM will need to align with zero trust frameworks by ensuring that identity data remains accurate and up to date in real time. Continuous identity synchronization between identity providers, endpoint security systems, and access control mechanisms will be critical for enforcing zero trust policies. Future SCIM implementations may also integrate with identity threat detection systems to enable proactive risk assessments based on user behavior and contextual factors.

Artificial intelligence and machine learning are set to play an increasingly important role in identity management. AI-driven identity analytics can detect anomalies, automate access decisions, and enhance fraud prevention by analyzing patterns in user behavior. SCIM can support AI-powered identity management by providing a standardized data model for user attributes and access changes. By feeding SCIM-synchronized identity data into AI-driven security platforms, organizations can gain deeper insights into potential security threats and automate responses to identity-related risks. The integration of SCIM with AI will enable organizations to improve identity governance by dynamically adjusting access privileges based on risk assessments and behavioral analytics.

As cloud adoption continues to rise, the need for identity synchronization across cloud-based applications and hybrid environments is becoming increasingly complex. Organizations are leveraging a mix of Software as a Service (SaaS), Platform as a Service (PaaS), and on-premises systems, creating a fragmented identity landscape. SCIM provides a unified framework for managing identities across these diverse environments, ensuring that user accounts, roles, and permissions remain consistent across all platforms. The future of SCIM will involve enhancements that improve its scalability, allowing organizations to manage millions of users across multi-cloud environments with minimal latency. Cloud-native SCIM implementations will need to optimize API performance, support event-driven architectures, and integrate with containerized identity services to handle the growing complexity of identity synchronization.

Another significant development in identity management is the growing emphasis on privacy and compliance. Regulations such as GDPR, CCPA, and other data protection laws require organizations to implement strict controls over how user identity data is collected, stored, and shared. SCIM can help organizations maintain compliance by enforcing standardized identity management practices and ensuring that user data is consistently updated and removed when necessary. Future iterations of SCIM may incorporate built-in privacy controls that allow users to manage their consent preferences, determine how their identity data is shared, and request the deletion of their information across all integrated systems. SCIM implementations may also include automated compliance reporting features to help organizations demonstrate adherence to data protection regulations.

The adoption of passwordless authentication is another area where SCIM will play a key role. As organizations move away from traditional passwords in favor of biometric authentication, hardware security keys, and multi-factor authentication (MFA), identity synchronization must support these modern authentication methods. SCIM will need to evolve to handle new authentication mechanisms, ensuring that identity attributes related to passwordless authentication are consistently managed across all connected applications. By enabling organizations to synchronize authentication methods across their identity infrastructure, SCIM will contribute to the broader shift toward stronger and more user-friendly authentication experiences.

SCIM's role in access governance is also expected to expand. Identity governance and administration (IGA) solutions rely on identity synchronization to enforce policies, conduct access reviews, and ensure least-privilege access. SCIM will continue to be a critical component of access governance frameworks by providing real-time updates on user entitlements and access changes. Future SCIM developments may introduce enhanced auditing capabilities, enabling organizations to track historical identity changes and generate reports that demonstrate compliance with governance policies. Integration with identity risk assessment tools will allow organizations to dynamically adjust user access based on contextual risk factors.

Interoperability with emerging identity protocols and standards will be essential for SCIM's continued success. The identity landscape is evolving with the adoption of OpenID Connect, FIDO2, Verifiable Credentials, and other authentication and authorization standards. SCIM will need to maintain compatibility with these protocols to ensure seamless integration across identity ecosystems. Future SCIM implementations may include support for exchanging identity data with verifiable credential systems, allowing organizations to verify user identities without relying on centralized databases. This interoperability will be crucial for enabling seamless digital identity interactions across different industries and sectors.

As organizations continue to prioritize automation, efficiency, and security in identity management, SCIM will remain a cornerstone of modern identity synchronization strategies. By evolving alongside advancements in decentralized identity, zero trust security, AI-driven analytics, and compliance frameworks, SCIM will play a vital role in shaping the future of identity management. Its adaptability, scalability, and interoperability will ensure that organizations can effectively manage identities across complex, dynamic environments while meeting the growing demands of security, privacy, and regulatory compliance.

Comparing SCIM with Other Identity Protocols

SCIM (System for Cross-domain Identity Management) is one of many identity management protocols used to facilitate user provisioning, synchronization, and deprovisioning across different systems. While SCIM provides a standardized and automated approach to identity lifecycle management, other identity protocols serve distinct purposes in authentication, authorization, and access control. Comparing SCIM with protocols such as LDAP, SAML, OAuth, and OpenID Connect highlights the strengths and limitations of each approach, as well as how they can complement each other in a comprehensive identity management strategy.

LDAP (Lightweight Directory Access Protocol) is one of the oldest and most widely used protocols for managing and retrieving directory-based identity information. It provides a hierarchical structure for storing user attributes and access policies, making it a fundamental component of many enterprise identity directories, such as Microsoft Active Directory and OpenLDAP. Unlike SCIM, which focuses on identity provisioning and synchronization across multiple applications, LDAP primarily serves as a directory service for querying and managing identity data within a centralized repository. One of LDAP's advantages is its efficiency in handling large-scale directory lookups, but it lacks a built-in mechanism for automated user provisioning across cloud applications. SCIM addresses this gap by enabling seamless identity synchronization between on-premises directories and cloud-based identity providers, ensuring that user attributes remain up to date across all systems.

SAML (Security Assertion Markup Language) is another widely used identity protocol that serves a different purpose than SCIM. While

SCIM focuses on identity provisioning and management, SAML is designed for single sign-on (SSO) and federated authentication. SAML enables users to authenticate once with an identity provider and access multiple applications without needing to re-enter their credentials. It uses XML-based assertions to communicate authentication and authorization decisions between identity providers and service providers. Unlike SCIM, SAML does not handle user provisioning or attribute synchronization, meaning that user accounts must already exist in target applications before authentication can occur. SCIM and SAML often work together in enterprise environments, with SCIM managing user accounts and attributes while SAML handles secure authentication and authorization.

OAuth (Open Authorization) is another identity protocol that differs significantly from SCIM in terms of functionality. OAuth is designed for delegated authorization, allowing applications to access user resources on behalf of the user without exposing their credentials. It is commonly used in scenarios where third-party applications need limited access to a user's account, such as granting a mobile app permission to access a cloud storage service. Unlike SCIM, which focuses on identity lifecycle management, OAuth provides a secure framework for granting and revoking access tokens based on user consent. OAuth is often used alongside SCIM to ensure that user attributes are properly provisioned and synchronized before access tokens are issued, ensuring that only valid and authorized users receive access to protected resources.

OpenID Connect (OIDC) builds on top of OAuth 2.0 to provide authentication capabilities, allowing applications to verify a user's identity and obtain identity attributes from an identity provider. OIDC is widely used for federated authentication in modern applications, enabling seamless sign-in experiences across multiple services. While OIDC facilitates authentication, it does not handle identity provisioning or lifecycle management, making it complementary to SCIM. Organizations often integrate SCIM with OIDC to ensure that authenticated users have up-to-date attributes and access rights before logging into an application. This integration helps maintain consistency between authentication events and identity records, reducing the risk of access discrepancies.

Another identity management standard that is often compared to SCIM is Just-in-Time (JIT) provisioning. JIT provisioning allows user accounts to be created on-demand when a user logs in through an identity provider. Unlike SCIM, which proactively synchronizes identity data between systems, JIT provisioning occurs dynamically during authentication, reducing the need for pre-existing user accounts in target applications. While JIT provisioning can simplify access management in some cases, it lacks the ability to synchronize ongoing user attribute changes, making it less effective for organizations that require real-time updates across multiple applications. SCIM provides a more comprehensive solution for managing user lifecycle events, ensuring that changes such as role updates and account deactivations are consistently propagated.

In cloud-native environments, organizations often use a combination of SCIM, OIDC, and OAuth to manage authentication, authorization, and identity synchronization. SCIM ensures that user attributes are provisioned and synchronized across cloud applications, OIDC handles authentication and identity verification, and OAuth manages delegated authorization. This combination allows organizations to implement a secure and scalable identity management framework that meets the needs of modern applications and distributed architectures.

One of the challenges organizations face when implementing identity protocols is ensuring interoperability between different systems. While SCIM provides a standardized REST-based API for user provisioning, not all applications natively support SCIM. Some legacy systems still rely on LDAP, while others require proprietary connectors for identity synchronization. Organizations must carefully evaluate their identity landscape to determine the best approach for integrating SCIM with existing protocols. In some cases, middleware solutions or identity brokers can bridge the gap between SCIM and non-SCIM-compliant applications, enabling seamless identity synchronization.

Security considerations also play a crucial role in selecting identity protocols. While SCIM provides secure identity provisioning, it must be implemented with strong authentication mechanisms to prevent unauthorized access to user data. OAuth and OIDC provide robust mechanisms for securing API access and authentication flows, making them essential components of a secure identity management strategy.

Organizations should enforce best practices such as using strong encryption, multi-factor authentication, and role-based access control to enhance security across all identity protocols.

Compliance requirements also influence the choice of identity protocols. Many regulations, such as GDPR, HIPAA, and CCPA, mandate strict controls over user data management and access. SCIM helps organizations maintain compliance by ensuring that user data is consistently updated and removed when necessary. When combined with other identity protocols, such as SAML for secure authentication and OAuth for controlled access delegation, SCIM provides a comprehensive framework for meeting regulatory requirements.

While SCIM serves a distinct purpose in identity lifecycle management, it is most effective when used in conjunction with other identity protocols. LDAP remains relevant for directory-based authentication, SAML provides federated SSO, OAuth enables delegated authorization, and OIDC facilitates identity verification. Organizations that leverage SCIM alongside these protocols can create a seamless and secure identity management ecosystem that supports modern authentication, authorization, and identity provisioning needs. By understanding the strengths and limitations of each protocol, organizations can design an identity architecture that optimally balances security, efficiency, and interoperability.

SCIM for Internet of Things (IoT)

The rapid growth of the Internet of Things (IoT) has introduced new challenges in identity and access management. IoT ecosystems consist of a vast number of connected devices, sensors, and applications that require secure authentication and authorization. Unlike traditional IT environments, where identity management is focused on users and enterprise applications, IoT expands identity management to include non-human entities such as smart devices, industrial sensors, and autonomous systems. SCIM (System for Cross-domain Identity Management), originally designed for user provisioning and synchronization, is now being explored as a solution for managing the identity lifecycle of IoT devices. By adapting SCIM for IoT, organizations can automate device onboarding, enforce access policies, and improve the security and scalability of IoT networks.

One of the key challenges in IoT identity management is provisioning and deprovisioning devices at scale. Large IoT deployments often involve thousands or even millions of devices that need to be securely registered, assigned attributes, and granted appropriate access permissions. Manual provisioning methods are impractical for such large-scale operations, leading to inefficiencies and potential security risks. SCIM can streamline this process by providing an automated mechanism for registering IoT devices with identity providers. Just as SCIM provisions user accounts in enterprise applications, it can be extended to provision device identities, ensuring that each device is properly authenticated and configured upon deployment.

Managing device attributes and metadata is another critical aspect of IoT identity management. IoT devices often have unique attributes such as device type, firmware version, location, and operational status. These attributes must be consistently synchronized across identity management systems, security platforms, and IoT gateways. SCIM's standardized schema can be extended to accommodate device-specific attributes, allowing organizations to maintain an accurate and up-to-date inventory of all connected devices. This ensures that security policies and access controls are based on real-time device information, reducing the risk of unauthorized access due to outdated records.

Access control in IoT environments requires a dynamic and automated approach. Unlike user identities, which are relatively static, IoT devices frequently change their network locations, roles, and operational states. SCIM can support dynamic access control by enabling real-time updates to device attributes and group memberships. For example, if a device is relocated to a different geographical region, SCIM can update its access permissions based on regional security policies. Similarly, if a device's firmware becomes outdated and poses a security risk, SCIM can trigger an automated restriction or quarantine process until the issue is resolved. This level of automation reduces the burden on IT administrators while enhancing the overall security posture of IoT networks.

Lifecycle management of IoT devices is another area where SCIM can provide significant benefits. IoT devices have varying lifespans, with some requiring frequent replacements, upgrades, or decommissioning. Failing to properly deprovision retired devices can lead to security vulnerabilities, as abandoned identities may be exploited by malicious actors. SCIM can automate the deprovisioning process by ensuring that decommissioned devices are removed from identity directories and access control lists in real time. This helps prevent unauthorized access by devices that are no longer in use and maintains compliance with security policies.

Interoperability is a major challenge in IoT identity management due to the diverse range of device manufacturers, protocols, and communication standards. SCIM's REST-based architecture makes it well-suited for integration with various IoT platforms, identity providers, and security frameworks. By implementing SCIM-compatible identity management solutions, organizations can achieve seamless interoperability across different IoT environments without relying on proprietary identity synchronization mechanisms. Standardizing IoT identity management with SCIM also simplifies compliance with industry regulations that mandate strong identity and access controls for connected devices.

Security concerns in IoT extend beyond traditional user authentication to include device authentication, authorization, and secure communication. SCIM can complement existing security frameworks by ensuring that only trusted devices are granted access to IoT networks. When combined with authentication mechanisms such as mutual TLS, OAuth, or certificate-based authentication, SCIM can help enforce strong identity verification for IoT devices. Additionally, SCIM's support for role-based access control (RBAC) can be extended to IoT environments, allowing devices to be grouped into different roles with predefined permissions. This ensures that devices only have access to the resources necessary for their function, minimizing the risk of unauthorized actions.

The scalability of SCIM makes it an attractive option for IoT deployments that involve large numbers of connected devices. Traditional identity management systems may struggle to handle the high-volume identity transactions required in IoT networks. SCIM's lightweight, JSON-based data model and RESTful API design enable efficient identity synchronization at scale. By leveraging SCIM for IoT identity management, organizations can handle the dynamic nature of IoT environments while ensuring optimal performance and reliability.

The integration of SCIM with artificial intelligence and machine learning can further enhance IoT security and management. AI-driven analytics can detect abnormal device behavior and trigger SCIM-based identity updates in response to potential threats. For instance, if an IoT security system identifies a device behaving suspiciously, it can use SCIM to automatically revoke the device's access privileges or move it to a restricted security group. This level of automation helps organizations respond to security threats in real time, reducing the risk of IoT-related cyberattacks.

Compliance and regulatory requirements are becoming increasingly stringent for IoT security and identity management. Many industries, including healthcare, finance, and critical infrastructure, must adhere to strict security standards that require strong identity governance for connected devices. SCIM can assist organizations in meeting compliance requirements by maintaining accurate identity records, enforcing access policies, and providing audit logs of identity-related changes. By leveraging SCIM as part of an IoT identity governance framework, organizations can enhance transparency and accountability in their IoT security practices.

The adoption of SCIM for IoT identity management represents a step toward creating a more secure, scalable, and interoperable IoT ecosystem. As IoT networks continue to expand and evolve, identity management solutions must adapt to handle the growing complexity of connected devices. By extending SCIM's capabilities to support device identities, organizations can improve automation, enhance security, and simplify compliance in IoT environments. As the industry moves toward a more standardized approach to IoT identity management, SCIM is likely to play an increasingly important role in ensuring the integrity and security of connected devices worldwide.

Open Source SCIM Implementations

SCIM (System for Cross-domain Identity Management) has become a widely adopted standard for automating user identity provisioning and synchronization across various applications and platforms. While many commercial identity providers and cloud services offer SCIM-based integrations, open source SCIM implementations provide organizations with flexible and cost-effective solutions for managing identity synchronization. Open source SCIM servers and clients enable organizations to build customized identity management solutions, integrate with existing infrastructure, and contribute to the broader SCIM ecosystem. These implementations are particularly beneficial for enterprises that require greater control over identity management, want to avoid vendor lock-in, or need to extend SCIM functionality to meet specific requirements.

One of the most widely used open source SCIM implementations is SimpleSCIM, a lightweight and flexible SCIM server written in Java. SimpleSCIM provides a minimalistic SCIM 2.0 implementation that organizations can deploy in their environments to handle user provisioning and deprovisioning. It supports common SCIM operations, including user and group management, attribute filtering, and bulk updates. SimpleSCIM is particularly useful for developers looking to integrate SCIM functionality into existing identity management solutions without adding unnecessary complexity. Its REST-based architecture allows easy integration with various identity providers and authentication services, making it a practical choice for organizations that want to implement SCIM without relying on commercial offerings.

Another popular open source SCIM solution is SCIMple, a SCIM 2.0-compliant framework developed in Python. SCIMple provides both client and server implementations, enabling organizations to either expose SCIM endpoints for identity synchronization or integrate SCIM functionality into their existing applications. With its modular design, SCIMple allows developers to customize user and group provisioning workflows, making it suitable for enterprises that require tailored identity management solutions. The framework's Python-based implementation makes it an attractive choice for organizations that already use Python for their identity and access management (IAM) systems.

Gluu SCIM is another notable open source SCIM implementation, built as part of the Gluu IAM platform. Gluu is an open source identity provider that supports authentication, authorization, and identity federation. Its SCIM module extends identity management capabilities by providing standardized user provisioning and deprovisioning features. Organizations using Gluu for identity management can leverage its SCIM functionality to synchronize user identities with external applications and cloud services. The integration of SCIM with Gluu's existing authentication and access control mechanisms allows for a more comprehensive IAM strategy, ensuring that user attributes remain consistent across multiple systems.

Apache Syncope is an open source identity management solution that includes SCIM support as part of its broader IAM capabilities. Apache Syncope provides identity provisioning, access control, and governance features, making it a suitable choice for enterprises that need a fully-fledged IAM solution with SCIM integration. By supporting SCIM 2.0, Apache Syncope enables organizations to automate user and group management across various applications, reducing administrative overhead and improving security. The extensibility of Apache Syncope allows organizations to define custom attributes, enforce access policies, and integrate with external authentication providers while maintaining SCIM compliance.

One of the advantages of using open source SCIM implementations is the ability to customize identity synchronization processes. Many organizations have unique identity management requirements that commercial SCIM solutions may not fully address. Open source SCIM implementations allow developers to modify source code, extend functionality, and optimize performance based on specific use cases. This flexibility is particularly valuable for organizations operating in regulated industries where strict compliance requirements necessitate custom identity management solutions.

Security is a crucial aspect of SCIM implementations, and open source solutions provide transparency by allowing organizations to audit code and apply security best practices. Unlike proprietary SCIM solutions, where security vulnerabilities may not be immediately disclosed, open source SCIM projects benefit from community contributions and peer-reviewed code. Organizations can implement additional security measures such as role-based access control (RBAC), multi-factor authentication (MFA), and encryption to enhance the security of SCIM endpoints. Regular updates from open source communities also ensure that security patches and performance improvements are continuously integrated.

Scalability is another factor to consider when choosing an open source SCIM implementation. Some open source SCIM servers are designed for small to medium-sized deployments, while others can scale to support enterprise-level identity synchronization. Organizations with large user bases must evaluate SCIM implementations based on their ability to handle high-volume identity transactions efficiently. Load balancing, caching mechanisms, and database optimizations can help improve the performance of open source SCIM deployments in large-scale environments.

Integration with existing identity providers and authentication services is a key consideration when adopting open source SCIM solutions. Many organizations already use identity platforms such as Microsoft Active Directory, Okta, Keycloak, or Google Workspace for authentication and access management. Open source SCIM implementations can serve as intermediaries between these identity providers and third-party applications, ensuring seamless identity synchronization. By leveraging SCIM's standardized API, organizations can reduce the complexity of integrating disparate identity systems, enabling a more unified and automated identity management framework.

Organizations considering open source SCIM implementations should also evaluate community support and documentation. While open source projects provide cost-effective alternatives to commercial SCIM solutions, the availability of community support, active development, and detailed documentation can impact adoption success. Projects with active developer communities, well-maintained repositories, and responsive forums are more likely to receive regular updates, security patches, and feature enhancements. Organizations should assess the long-term viability of open source SCIM implementations to ensure continued support and compatibility with evolving identity management needs.

Testing and validation are essential before deploying an open source SCIM implementation in a production environment. Organizations should conduct thorough testing to verify compliance with SCIM 2.0 specifications, ensure data consistency, and evaluate API performance under various conditions. Automated testing frameworks and API validation tools can help identify potential issues before deployment.

By simulating real-world identity synchronization scenarios, organizations can fine-tune their SCIM configurations and mitigate risks associated with incorrect provisioning, attribute mismatches, or security vulnerabilities.

Adopting an open source SCIM implementation offers organizations a cost-effective and flexible approach to identity synchronization while maintaining control over their identity management infrastructure. By leveraging community-driven SCIM solutions, organizations can customize provisioning workflows, integrate with existing IAM systems, and enhance security through transparent code audits. As identity management continues to evolve, open source SCIM implementations will remain a valuable resource for enterprises looking to automate and standardize identity synchronization across their digital ecosystems.

Conclusion and Next Steps

The adoption of SCIM (System for Cross-domain Identity Management) has transformed how organizations manage user identities across applications, cloud services, and on-premises systems. By providing a standardized, automated approach to identity provisioning and synchronization, SCIM reduces administrative burden, improves security, and ensures that identity data remains consistent across an organization's ecosystem. As businesses continue to embrace digital transformation, SCIM has become a critical component of modern identity management strategies, supporting seamless integration with identity providers, SaaS applications, and enterprise systems.

One of the key benefits of SCIM is its ability to simplify user lifecycle management. Traditional identity management solutions often rely on manual processes, custom scripts, or proprietary APIs that require ongoing maintenance and create potential security gaps. SCIM eliminates these challenges by offering a common protocol for user and group management, enabling organizations to automatically provision and deprovision accounts based on real-time changes in their identity provider or HR system. This level of automation helps organizations enforce access policies, prevent orphaned accounts, and ensure compliance with regulatory requirements.

Security remains a top priority in identity management, and SCIM plays a vital role in strengthening an organization's security posture. By ensuring that user attributes, roles, and group memberships are consistently synchronized, SCIM reduces the risk of unauthorized access to sensitive applications. When integrated with authentication protocols such as OAuth, OpenID Connect, and SAML, SCIM enables a secure and seamless user experience while maintaining centralized control over identity data. Organizations that implement SCIM alongside security best practices, such as multi-factor authentication (MFA) and zero trust architecture, can enhance their overall security strategy and reduce identity-related threats.

Scalability is another significant advantage of SCIM. As organizations grow and expand their IT environments, managing thousands or even millions of user accounts across multiple platforms can become overwhelming. SCIM's lightweight and RESTful architecture allows organizations to handle large-scale identity synchronization efficiently, making it an ideal solution for enterprises, SaaS providers, and cloud-based environments. Whether managing employee identities within an enterprise or synchronizing customer accounts across a digital platform, SCIM provides a scalable foundation for identity management.

Despite the benefits of SCIM, organizations must take strategic steps to ensure a successful implementation. Proper planning, schema design, and attribute mapping are essential to avoid compatibility issues and data inconsistencies. Organizations should conduct a thorough assessment of their existing identity infrastructure, define clear provisioning and deprovisioning policies, and test SCIM integrations in a controlled environment before deploying them at scale. By following best practices and leveraging open source or commercial SCIM implementations, organizations can minimize risks and achieve a smooth transition to SCIM-based identity management.

One of the common challenges in SCIM adoption is ensuring interoperability with existing identity solutions. Many enterprises use a combination of legacy directory services, cloud identity providers, and proprietary identity management platforms. While SCIM provides a standardized framework, not all applications natively support SCIM out of the box. Organizations may need to develop custom connectors, leverage identity brokers, or use middleware solutions to bridge the gap between SCIM-compliant and non-compliant systems. Investing in flexible identity orchestration tools can help organizations achieve seamless SCIM integration across their entire IT ecosystem.

As identity management continues to evolve, SCIM is expected to play a growing role in enabling next-generation identity solutions. Emerging trends such as decentralized identity, verifiable credentials, and passwordless authentication will shape the future of identity management, requiring identity synchronization mechanisms that can support new identity models. SCIM's extensibility allows organizations to define custom attributes and extend its capabilities to meet the demands of modern identity frameworks. By staying informed about SCIM advancements and industry trends, organizations can future-proof their identity management strategies and ensure long-term success.

Organizations looking to implement SCIM should take a phased approach to deployment. Starting with a small pilot project allows teams to validate SCIM configurations, test interoperability with existing applications, and identify potential challenges before scaling up. Once a successful proof of concept is established, organizations can gradually expand SCIM adoption across departments, applications, and third-party services. Continuous monitoring, logging, and security assessments should be implemented to detect and mitigate potential identity synchronization issues.

Collaboration with industry peers, standards organizations, and the SCIM open source community can also enhance an organization's SCIM implementation. Many enterprises contribute to SCIM development efforts, share best practices, and provide feedback on improving the standard. Engaging with SCIM working groups, attending identity management conferences, and participating in developer forums can help organizations stay up to date with the latest developments and optimize their SCIM deployment for maximum efficiency and security.

Training and documentation are crucial for successful SCIM adoption. IT administrators, developers, and security teams should receive proper training on SCIM concepts, API usage, and troubleshooting techniques. Comprehensive documentation should be maintained to outline SCIM schema definitions, provisioning workflows, error handling processes, and integration guidelines. Providing clear documentation helps ensure that SCIM remains a well-managed and sustainable identity management solution over time.

Moving forward, organizations should evaluate their identity management roadmap and determine how SCIM fits into their broader IAM strategy. Whether integrating SCIM with identity governance platforms, cloud-based access management solutions, or emerging identity technologies, organizations should continuously refine their approach to identity synchronization. As digital transformation accelerates and identity security becomes more critical, SCIM will continue to serve as a foundational component of automated and scalable identity management.

By taking proactive steps to implement, optimize, and maintain SCIM, organizations can achieve a more secure, efficient, and standardized approach to identity provisioning. The journey to effective identity management does not end with SCIM adoption—it requires ongoing monitoring, adaptation to new security challenges, and integration with evolving identity frameworks. With the right strategy in place, SCIM can help organizations build a resilient and future-proof identity management infrastructure that supports business growth and security in an increasingly interconnected digital landscape.

www.ingramcontent.com/pod-product-compliance
Lightning Source LLC
LaVergne TN
LVHW022317060326
832902LV00020B/3526